THE PEOPLE OF THE NIGHT TAROT COMPENDIUM

PRESENTED BY ʿĀʾISHAH BINT MANIYYAH

"THE PEOPLE OF THE NIGHT ARE GIVEN IN THE DARKNESS WHAT IS NOT GIVEN IN THE LIGHT."

— AḤMAD AL-BŪNĪ, SHAMS AL-MAʿĀRIF AL-KUBRĀ (BEINECKE MS 32304220, FOL. 54A)[1]

THE PEOPLE OF THE NIGHT TAROT COMPENDIUM

Presented by ʿĀʾishah bint Maniyyah

Published by Ash-Shiʿra Publishing
First Edition, 2026

Card Artwork generated in collaboration with Grok, built by xAI.
Inspired by the Rider-Waite-Smith Tarot, Crowley-Harris Thoth Tarot, and Islamicate mystical traditions including Aḥmad al-Būnī and Muḥyī al-Dīn Ibn al-ʿArabī.

ISBN: 979-8-9954396-0-8

For Inquiries: ashshira@usa.com

ALHAMDULILLAH

~ ALL PRAISE IS DUE TO ALLAH

THE SHEMA ~ JEWISH DECLARATION OF FAITH
DEUTERONOMY 6:4 (KJV)
SHEMA YISROEL ADONAI ELOHEINU ADONAI ECHAD
HEAR, O ISRAEL: THE LORD OUR GOD IS ONE LORD

1 CORINTHIANS 8:6 (KJV)
BUT TO US THERE IS BUT ONE GOD, THE FATHER, OF
WHOM ARE ALL THINGS, AND WE IN HIM; AND ONE LORD
JESUS CHRIST, BY WHOM ARE ALL THINGS, AND WE BY
HIM.

THE SHAHADA ~ ISLAMIC TESTIMONY OF FAITH
ASHHADU AN LĀ ILĀHA ILLĀ ALLĀH, WA ASHHADU ANNA
MUḥAMMADAN RASŪLU ALLĀH.
I BEAR WITNESS THAT THERE IS NO GOD BUT ALLAH, AND
I BEAR WITNESS THAT MUHAMMAD IS THE MESSENGER OF
ALLAH.

THIS WORK IS DEDICATED TO DUTCH AND CUB

SPECIAL THANKS TO MY TEACHER AND ALL THOSE THAT HELPED ALONG THE WAY

CONTENTS

INTRODUCTION

The People of the Night Tarot draws deeply upon The Rider-Waite-Smith Tarot (RWS) and The Crowley-Harris Thoth Tarot for overall structure, iconography and formatting though was also inspired by their predecessors such as the Marseille Tarot and Visconti-Sforza Tarrocchi decks. For content and flavor specific to The People of the Night Tarot we drew heavily from mystical streams originating in the Islamicate tradition as well as from the shadow side of the unconscious - reflected upon as the light of the moon shimmers over dark waters. The namesake of The People of the Night Tarot was based upon an excerpt from an ancient manuscript entitled the '*Shams al-Ma'arif (the Sun of Knowledge)*' attributed to the infamous mystic and scholar Ahmad al-Būnī whose work has inspired both fear and intrigue within the Islamicate world for centuries. The adapted passage can be translated something akin to: "The

People of the Night are given in the darkness what is not given in the light."[1]

DECK STRUCTURE

While the order and card titles closely align to the RWS format; the zodiacal, elementary, planetary, and Hebrew letter attributions as well as many of the Hermetic titles of the cards with origins in Thelemic and Golden Dawn magical traditions as utilized by the Thoth Tarot were also incorporated. Also, in addition to the Hebrew letter attributions for the major arcana, their numerical values in both standard and final letter forms have also been added, along with the corresponding Arabic letters sharing those same values. Having built upon these pillars of Western esoteric tradition, The People of the Night Tarot also drank from currents originating in the Islamicate tradition, primarily from the renowned Sufi mystics and scholars Ahmad al-Būnī (al-Būnī) and Muḥyī al-Dīn Ibn al-ʿArabī (Ibn ʿArabī).

The court cards contain much of their traditional Western nomenclature though with minor variations. In the RWS system the titles were King, Queen, Knight, and Page; whereas in the Thoth system the titles Knight, Queen, Prince, and Princess were utilized. We took somewhat of a middle path approach in this regard labeling them as King, Queen, Prince, and Princess. Additionally, certain of the divine names of God along with a corresponding verse from the Quran were also attributed to the court cards based upon an interpretation of the names and verses relating to traditional card qualities. For instance, with the King of Wands retaining the traditional association of being the Fiery (King) part of Fire (Wands), the Queen of Wands being the Watery (Queen) part of Fire (Wands), and so on - where Kings and Wands relate to Fire, Queens and Cups to Water, Princes and Swords to Air, and Princesses and Pentacles to Earth - The People of the Night Tarot incorporated a divine name and Quranic verse sharing similar elemental qualities. Hence, the King of Wands was provided with the name Al-Qahhār ~ The Subduer, The Irresistible, The Overwhelming Conqueror; and the verse chosen was Surah Ta-Ha 20:111 (Pickthall) "And faces shall be humbled before the Living, the Self-Subsisting. And indeed he fails who carries wrongdoing."

In a similar fashion, the Aces of each of the suits that have oft been associated with the seasons - such as Pentacles ~ Spring, Wands ~ Summer, Cups ~ Fall, Swords ~ Winter - were assigned corresponding Archangels - Isrāfīl (Raphael), Mīkā'īl (Michael), Jibrīl (Gabriel), and ʿAzrā'īl (Azrael) - each with an accompanying related verse from the Quran. For example, the Angel Isrāfīl was attributed to the Ace of Pentacles and Spring along with the corresponding verse: Surah Az-Zumar 39:68 (Pickthall) "And the trumpet is blown, and all who are in the heavens and all who are in the earth swoon, save him whom Allah willeth. Then it is blown a second time, and lo! they stand up, looking on." In this instance the Angel and verse may relate to the resurrection of spring following the death of winter drawing parallels to the symbolism of the Vernal Equinox. Please note that different attributions exist depending on system, practitioner, etc.

Finally, for the pip cards numbered two through ten that Western tradition often affiliates with the zodiacal decans - each of the 12 zodiacal signs, Aries through Pisces, being comprised of three decans where each decan consists of ten degrees producing a total of 36 decans in the 360° zodiacal wheel - we retained a similar structure though incorporated features from the Islamicate tradition as well. Specifically, each day of the moon's approximately 28 day cycle that it takes to navigate the entire zodiacal wheel is attributed to a lunar mansion consisting of approximately 12° 51' - 12 degrees and 51 minutes - and each of these 28 lunar mansions have been introduced into the pip cards' format.

The method applied for the placement of the lunar mansions within the deck is as follows: for each mansion that begins in a specific decan, the mansion name - the name being provided in Arabic on the cards themselves though for English rendering, meaning, and further mansion details please see the table provided in the Lunar Mansions chapter - and starting point - in degree and minutes - is provided. In certain decans where no new mansion begins, the starting point of the mansion that the card still lies in is provided. For example, the lunar mansion Al-Balda begins in the second decan of Sagittarius - the Nine of Wands - with a starting point of 17° 8'. No new mansion starts in the third decan of Sagittarius - the Ten of Wands - so the same mansion name and starting point that began in the prior decan are again provided. Whether one is utilizing the People of the Night Tarot for the purposes of divination -

which some may view as haram/forbidden - or for meditative type practices, these additional card prompts may be utilized for further contemplation, consideration, journeying, and or reflection.

ASTROLOGICAL WHEEL

An astrological correspondence wheel has been included in this compendium as a quick reference tool for readings. In regards to the formatting of the wheel provided please observe the interplay between Islamicate and Western systems and take into account their inherent differences during your practice. While many in Western astrological circles utilize the Tropical zodiac, a large portion of astrologers from the Islamicate tradition employ the Sidereal. The difference between the Tropical and Sidereal systems pertains to where the actual planetary bodies are in the sky relative to where and in which zodiac sign their placement is attributed. For the Sidereal, the placement corresponds to where the planetary bodies actually are in the sky; whereas under the Tropical system the assignment is based upon their traditional placement. The difference between the tropical and sidereal systems has been termed the 'ayanamsa' and consists of approx. 24° 13' - 24 degrees and 13 minutes - as of early 2026

AD due to the precession of the equinoxes - a minor change in the angle of the earth's axis in relation to the fixed stars due to the earth's natural wobble. The shift amounts to approximately 1° every 72 years with a zero point - where Sidereal roughly equaled Tropical - somewhere around 285 AD. For the sake of simplicity and aesthetics, we have started both the Western traditional correspondences as well as those from the Islamicate tradition - primarily the lunar mansions - at 0° Aries though one may keep the Sidereal/Tropical variance in mind during application.

The wheel provided includes the 12 traditional zodiacal signs, the corresponding card numbers and associated decans, as well as the symbols for the related suits - for the suit of wands we substituted in a broomstick symbol, for cups a chalice, for swords a Japanese katana, and for pentacles a hexacle. The wheel has retained the traditional Golden Dawn planetary attributions for each of the decans provided in the Chaldean order and beginning with Mars at 0° Aries - Mars, Sun/Sol, Venus, Mercury, Moon/Luna, Saturn, and Jupiter. We have also included the ruling and exalted planets - if applicable - for each of the zodiacal signs read counterclockwise respectively.

If an exalted planet had not traditionally been associated with a sign a dash has been placed on the wheel in its stead. For the ruling and exalted planets we retained only the 7 classical planets. Please bear in mind, however, that some modern astrological systems incorporate the more recent discoveries and have Pluto ruling Scorpio, Uranus ruling Aquarius, and Neptune ruling Pisces.

The court cards have also retained their traditional placements with the queen encompassing the first two decans of the related cardinal sign - where Wands ~ Fire signs; Cups ~ Water Signs; Swords ~ Air signs; and Pentacles ~ Earth Signs; and where Aries, Cancer, Libra, and Capricorn are Cardinal/Initiatory; Leo, Scorpio, Aquarius, and Taurus are Kerubic/Fixed; and Sagittarius, Pisces, Gemini, and Virgo are Mutable - as well as the last decan of the previous sign; the Princes assuming the first two decans of the related Kerubic sign as well as the last decan of the prior sign; and the Kings encompassing the first two decans of the related mutable sign and the final decan from the prior sign.

The Aces and Princesses encompass the signs constituting their respective seasons and elemental associations where Aries, Taurus, and Gemini refer to Spring ~ Earth ~ Pentacles; Cancer, Leo, and

Virgo relate to Summer ~ Fire ~ Wands; Libra, Scorpio, and Sagittarius to Fall ~Water ~ Cups; and Capricorn, Aquarius, and Pisces constituting Winter ~ Air ~ Swords. Furthermore, the lunar mansions have been placed in the outer ring of the wheel written in Arabic script. For details regarding each of the mansions please reference the Lunar Mansions chapter. In addition to the wheel we have also included a table listing the average dates attributed to each decan. Please bear in mind that variation in dates and or attributions may be observed depending on source and time progression.

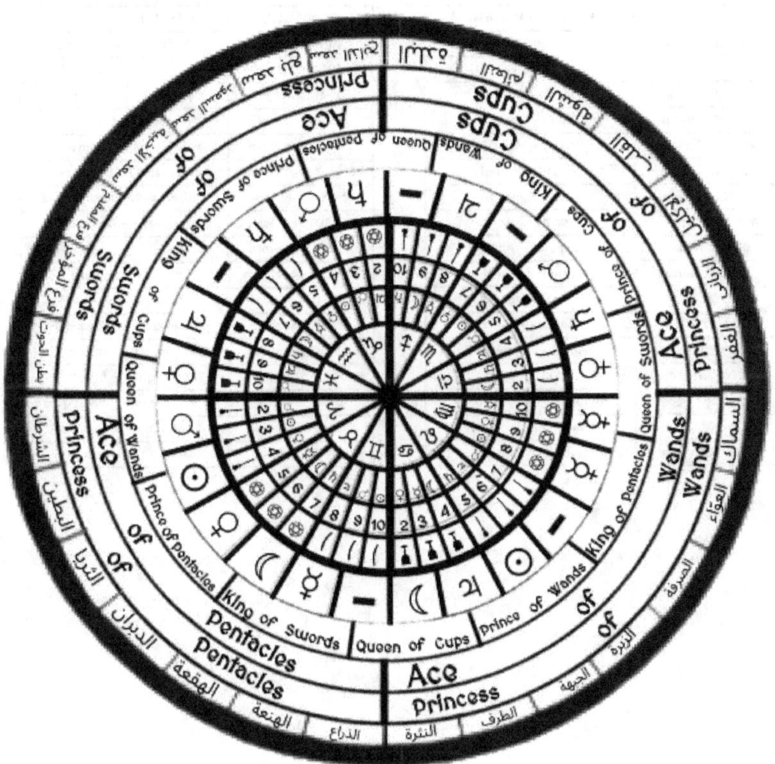

0°–10° Aries	March 21 – March 30		0°–10° Libra	September 23 – October 2
10°–20° Aries	March 31 – April 10		10°–20° Libra	October 3 – October 12
20°–30° Aries	April 11 – April 20		20°–30° Libra	October 13 – October 22
0°–10° Taurus	April 21 – April 30		0°–10° Scorpio	October 23 – November 2
10°–20° Taurus	May 1 – May 10		10°–20° Scorpio	November 3 – November 12
20°–30° Taurus	May 11 – May 20		20°–30° Scorpio	November 13 – November 22
0°–10° Gemini	May 21 – May 31		0°–10° Sagittarius	November 23 – December 2
10°–20° Gemini	June 1 – June 10		10°–20° Sagittarius	December 3 – December 12
20°–30° Gemini	June 11 – June 20		20°–30° Sagittarius	December 13 – December 21
0°–10° Cancer	June 21 – July 1		0°–10° Capricorn	December 22 – December 31
10°–20° Cancer	July 2 – July 11		10°–20° Capricorn	January 1 – January 10
20°–30° Cancer	July 12 – July 21		20°–30° Capricorn	January 11 – January 19
0°–10° Leo	July 22 – August 1		0°–10° Aquarius	January 20 – January 29
10°–20° Leo	August 2 – August 11		10°–20° Aquarius	January 30 – February 8
20°–30° Leo	August 12 – August 22		20°–30° Aquarius	February 9 – February 18
0°–10° Virgo	August 23 – September 1		0°–10° Pisces	February 19 – February 28
10°–20° Virgo	September 2 – September 11		10°–20° Pisces	March 1 – March 10
20°–30° Virgo	September 12 – September 22		20°–30° Pisces	March 11 – March 20

LUNAR MANSIONS

In accordance with The People of the Night Tarot's syncretic approach blending Western esoteric tradition with Judeo-Christian themes as well as incorporating those from the Islamicate realm; we have included a table containing motifs regarding the 28 Lunar Mansions previously mentioned in the Astrological Wheel chapter. While the Sun takes approximately 365 days to complete a cycle passing through each of the 12 zodiacal signs, the Moon - al-Qamar - finishes her cycle in approximately 28 days. In the Islamicate tradition a lunar mansion and its corresponding attributes have been assigned to each of these 28 days.

There are innumerable mysteries that surround the Moon. The ancients calculated that the distance from the Earth to the Moon was approximately 1/400 the distance from the Earth to the Sun and that the diameter of the Moon was approximately

1/400 of the diameter of the Sun - observations not far removed from modern measurements. This symmetry enables such even solar and lunar eclipses. The Moon has also been long connected to the oceanic tides as well as to a woman's roughly 28 day menstrual cycle. In addition to the lunar effect upon the waters of the ocean and its tides, the human body is composed of approximately 60% water and many posit that a similar effect as that on the tides also takes place within the human organism.

Mythology and common terminology also contain elements drawn from such lunar phenomena. From the werewolf that transforms under the full Moon to the terms 'lunacy' and 'lunatic' - from the Latin *Luna* - deriving their origins from the emotional impact that many cultures have attributed to the Moon's effects, as well as the term 'moonstruck' referring to someone in a lovestruck daze, the English language has been sprinkled with many such lunar roots. Although modern science may not directly be able to confirm such connections between emotional fluctuations and the Moon, they may be taking their measurements amidst a plethora of uncontrolled variables. For instance, modern lighting and screens, fast paced high stress lifestyles, hormone altering drugs, processed foods, dense populations, etc. could all be confounding factors that many living in ancient cultures would not have been encumbered by. So, while modern science may not entirely concur with such ancient observations regarding the emotional and or physical effects associated with the Moon, one could feasibly dispute the soundness of their argument.

Furthermore, deities spanning a wide range of cultures have been affiliated with the moon. Some of these include the Mesopotamian moon god Sin, the Greek goddesses Artemis and Selene, as well as Luna from the Roman pantheon in her full moon/mother aspect who was often syncretized with similar goddesses like Diana representing the waxing crescent/maiden phase and Hecate as the waning crescent/crone form of the triple goddess. Moreover, the Angel Jibreel/Gabriel - who delivered the Quran from Allah to the Prophet Muhammad ﷺ - has been connected with the Moon in the Islamicate tradition as well as in the Hebrew Qabalistic system, where Gabriel rules over the Sephirah Yesod, which is associated with the Moon.

Although only barely scratching the surface here regarding the enigma that is the Moon, we have included a table composed of attributions accorded to the 28 lunar mansions drawing from the Islamicate traditions of al-Būnī and Ibn ʿArabī. For each of the 28 mansions, we have included entries - or a dash if an entry is blank - for the mansion's name in Arabic as well as its English translation and transliteration. Although a star or stars have at some point been associated with each of the mansions, we decided to constrain the table here so as to only include some of the most unanimous and or classic star associations whilst leaving the others with only a dash mark. We also included the arabic letter relating to each of the mansions; at what point and in what sign each mansion starts in both degrees (°) and minutes (ʻ); as well as some general ascriptions such as which activities might serve beneficial to pursue while the moon is in said mansion as well as those to consider avoiding.

Additionally, we have included in the table one of the divine names of God that tradition has ascribed to each mansion. Please note that if reciting the divine name/s while the Moon is in the associated mansion - and or in general for Dhikr/Remembrance or calling upon the name in Dua/Supplication - one may substitute the definite article 'al' with a 'ya' to address the aspect beginning with an 'O...' rather than a 'the...'.

However, in the table we have listed the names in the traditional written format with the 'al' where applicable. Also, regarding the spelling of names - whether they be lunar mansion names, divine names, or others - utilized in this work and accompanying deck, the spellings have not always been static across sources. Spellings may differ for multiple reasons; whether they were simplified for ease of printing, incorporated into talismans, or drawn from different sources such as the Quran, grimoires, other manuscripts, etc. Please note that at times we have included more than one spelling variation.

Mansion:	Name:	Transliteration:	Meaning:	Main Star:	Arabic Letter:	Divine Name:	Begins:	Attributions:
1	الشرطان	al-Sharṭān	The Two Signs / The Horns	β Arietis (Sheratan)	ا	al-Fattāḥ الفتاح	0° Aries 00'	Good for beginnings, travel, marriage, planting; avoid lawsuits
2	البطين	al-Buṭayn	The Little Belly / The Dual Mark	—	ب	al-Razzāq الرزاق	12° 51' Aries	Good for business, hunting, water; avoid medical procedures
3	الثريا	al-Thurayyā	The Pleiades / The Little Cluster	Alcyone (η Tauri)	ج	al-Wahhāb الوهاب	25° 42' Aries	Very auspicious: love, marriage, planting, building
4	الدبران	al-Dabarān	The Follower / The Eye of Taurus	Aldebaran (α Tauri)	د	ar-Ra'ūf الرزوف	8° 34' Taurus	Good for building, travel; avoid partnerships
5	الهقعة	al-Haq'a	The White Spot / The Brand	—	ه	at-Tawwāb التواب	21° 25' Taurus	Good for love, healing; avoid new venture
6	الهنعة	al-Han'a	The Mark / The Brand	—	و	al-Muntaqim المنتقم	4° 17' Gemini	Good for travel, partnerships; avoid confrontations
7	الذراع	al-Dhirā'	The Forearm / The Lion's Paw	—	ز	al-'Azīz العزيز	17° 08' Gemini	Good for healing, love; avoid legal matters
8	النثرة	al-Nathra	The Gap / The Nostril	—	ح	al-Jabbār الجبار	0° Cancer 00'	Good for love, planting; avoid travel
9	الطرف	al-Ṭarf	The Glance / The Look	—	ط	al-Mutakabbir المتكبر	12° 51' Cancer	Good for healing, partnerships; avoid new projects
10	الجبهة	al-Jabha	The Forehead / The Mane	α Leonis (Regulus)	ي	al-Khāliq الخالق	25° 42' Cancer	Very auspicious: marriage, building, travel, planting
11	الزبرة	al-Zubra	The Mane / The Lion's Mane	—	ك	al-Bā'ith الباعث	8° 34' Leo	Good for partnerships, love; avoid confrontations
12	الصرفة	al-Ṣarfa	The Turn / The Change	—	ل	ash-Shahīd الشهيد	21° 25' Leo	Good for healing, travel; avoid marriage
13	العواء	al-'Awā	The Barking Dogs / The Howling	—	م	al-Majīd المجيد	4° 17' Virgo	Good for love, planting; avoid legal matters

No.	اسم المنزل	Transliteration	Meaning	Star	Letter	Divine Name	Position	Properties
14	السماك	al-Simāk	The Unarmed / The Lofty One	α Virginis (Spica)	ن	al-Bāsiṭ الباسط	17° 08' Virgo	Very auspicious: marriage, building, travel, healing
15	الغفر	al-Ghafr	The Covering / The Shield	—	س	ar-Rāziq الرازق	0° Libra 00'	Good for partnerships, love; avoid travel
16	الزبانى	al-Zubānā	The Claws / The Scorpion's Claws	α Librae (Zubenelgenubi)	ع	al-Fattāḥ الفتاح	12° 51' Libra	Good for healing, travel; avoid marriage
17	الإكليل	al-Iklīl	The Crown / The Wreath	—	ف	al-Wahhāb الوهاب	25° 42' Libra	Good for love, building; avoid confrontations
18	القلب	al-Qalb	The Heart	α Scorpii (Antares)	ص	ar-Ra'ūf الرؤوف	8° 34' Scorpio	Good for partnerships, healing; avoid legal matters
19	الشولة	al-Shawla	The Sting / The Raised Tail	—	ق	at-Tawwāb التواب	21° 25' Scorpio	Good for travel, love; avoid new projects
20	النعائم	al-Na'ā'im	The Ostriches / The Stars of the Camels	—	ر	al-Muntaqim المنتقم	4° 17' Sagittarius	Good for healing, partnerships; avoid marriage
21	البلدة	al-Balda	The City / The Empty Place	—	ش	al-'Azīz العزيز	17° 08' Sagittarius	Good for travel, love; avoid confrontations
22	سعد الذابح	Sa'd al-Dhābiḥ	The Lucky One of the Slaughterer	—	ت	al-Jabbār الجبار	0° Capricorn 00'	Good for healing, partnerships; avoid travel
23	سعد بلع	Sa'd Bula'	The Lucky One of the Swallower	—	ث	al-Mutakabbir المتكبر	12° 51' Capricorn	Good for love, building; avoid legal matters
24	سعد السعود	Sa'd al-Su'ūd	The Luckiest of the Lucky	—	ج	al-Khāliq الخالق	25° 42' Capricorn	Very auspicious: marriage, travel, planting
25	سعد الأخبية	Sa'd al-Akhbiya	The Lucky One of the Tents	—	ح	al-Bā'ith الباعث	8° 34' Aquarius	Good for partnerships, healing; avoid confrontations
26	الفرع المقدم	al-Fargh al-Muqaddam	The Fore Spout / The First Spout	α Pegasi (Markab)	خ	ash-Shahīd الشهيد	21° 25' Aquarius	Good for travel, love; avoid marriage
27	الفرع المؤخر	al-Fargh al-Mu'akhkhar	The Hind Spout / The Last Spout	—	ذ	al-Majīd المجيد	4° 17' Pisces	Good for healing, partnerships; avoid new projects
28	بطن الحوت	Baṭn al-Ḥūt	The Belly of the Fish	—	ظ	al-Bāsiṭ الباسط	17° 08' Pisces	Good for love, planting; avoid travel

TREE OF LIFE

The Qabalistic 'Tree of Life' - עֵץ הַחַיִּים ~ pronounced *Etz haChayim* or *Etz Chaim* - can be a diagrammatic representation of the process of creation via the descent of divine energy from the godhead down to the material realm as well as the ascent of the created back up the tree with the aim of unification with the godhead.

The tree is generally described with 32 components consisting of 10 sephiroth - energy centers - and 22 connecting paths between the Sephiroth. Each of the paths correlates to a letter from the Hebrew alphabet as well as to one of the 22 major arcana of the tarot. There are two main journeys often associated with the tree. One journey - often entitled the Path of the Lightning Flash or the Path of the Sword - is that which originates at the godhead and then emanates down the tree passing through each of the sephiroth in a zig zagging fashion. The other journey - often referred to as the Path of the Serpent or Path of Return/Ascension -

arises from the material realm then passes through the various 22 paths as it winds its way back up the tree.

On the tree diagram enclosed we retained the traditional Golden Dawn attributions and placed the names of the sephiroth - including the minor arcana cards associated with each- as well as the 22 paths and the corresponding major arcana card. For each of the 22 paths we also included the path number, Hebrew letter, letter meaning, and letter value. Even though not included on this diagram, please note that Aleister Crowley made a distinct change on the tree. Crowley's change was in accordance with his revelation that "Tzaddi is not the Star" originally given in the Thelemic sacred text *The Book of the Law (Liber AL vel Legis)*[2] though explained and implemented in his *The Book of Thoth.*[3] Crowley swapped the Emperor and Aries from path 15 - Chokmah to Tiphareth – with the Star and Aquarius from path 28 - Netzach to Yesod - though he left the letter Heh and letter Tzaddi in their original locations. So, as per Crowley, path 15 became associated with the letter Heh, the Star, and Aquarius; and Tzaddi, the Emperor, and Aries became attributed to path 28.

The tree has typically been assigned three main pillars: the right pillar, the left pillar, and the middle pillar which are termed the pillar of mercy, the pillar of severity, and the pillar of mildness - which could also be referred to as the straight or narrow path - respectively. In addition to the three pillars, the tree can also be divided into four main realms - also referred to as worlds. These sections have not always been divided up precisely the same though in accordance with common Golden Dawn literature, the sections could be assigned as follows: Atziluth ~ the archetypal realm, associated with the godhead and the element of Fire and comprised of the Supernals - which are the top three sephiroth - Kether, Chokhmah, and Binah; Briah ~ the mental realm associated with archangels and the element of water that is comprised of the sephiroth Chesed, Geburah, and Tiphareth; Yetzirah ~ the astral realm associated with angels and the element of air that is comprised of the sephiroth Netzach, Hod, and Yesod; and finally Assiah ~ the material realm associated with the physical universe and the element of earth that is comprised of the sephirah Malkuth.

Considering the four worlds in relation to the tree, one could interpret that there are infinite trees and that Malkuth on one tree could equate to Kether on the next tree down, and so on and so forth analogous to the biblical Jacob's Ladder - Genesis 28:12 (KJV) "And he dreamed, and behold a ladder set up on the earth, and the top of it reached to heaven: and behold the angels of God ascending and descending on it." Additionally, each of the worlds could be considered to have its own tree. So the tree in Atziluth - associated with fire - could be considered in the King scale; the tree in Briah - relating to water - would thus be in the Queen scale; that in Yetzirah - for air - in the Prince scale; and the tree of Malkuth - for earth - relating to the Princess scale. Although not elaborated upon here please bear in mind that each of these scales may also be appointed its own color schema.

For the purposes of this introduction regarding the tree of life, we have only briefly touched upon some basic tenets of a very complex subject. If one is interested in further study on the matter, we have included several excellent works in the Suggested Reading section near the end of the book. A few of the suggestions relevant here could be Aryeh Kaplan's *Sefer Yetzirah: The Book of Creation in Theory and Practice* regarding the tree in detail from a more traditional Jewish Kabalistic perspective; Chic and Tabitha Cicero's *Self Initiation into the Golden Dawn* for Golden Dawn specific materials; and Aleister Crowley's *The*

Book of Thoth' for a tarot specific focus that also delves into the unique alterations that Crowley incorporated into the tree and tarot for his system.

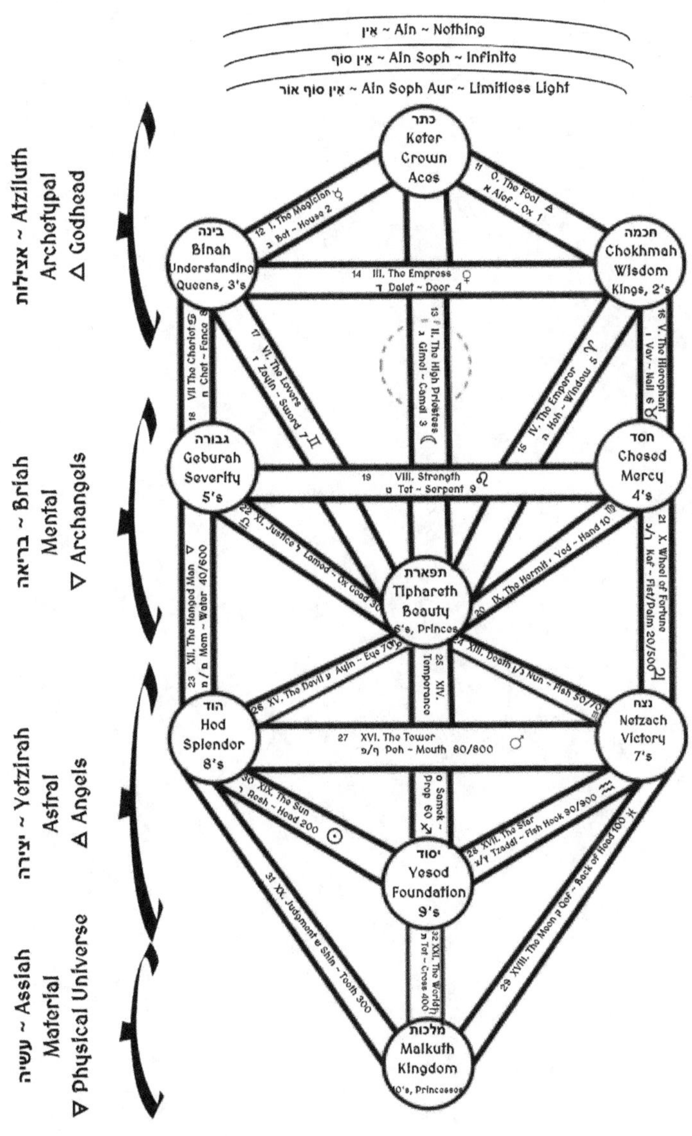

SETTING THE STAGE

Prior to a card reading, one may find it beneficial to adjust the space and build the atmosphere. If there is a candle or candles available one may light them and perhaps light some incense or burn essential resins as well. For readings, one may clean the reading surface with some Florida Water or similar simple cleansing and clearing product. In addition, a silk or satin cloth may be laid down to place the cards upon. Clearing the air by burning some palo santo or sweetgrass may also be desired. Lighting some mugwort incense or copal resin could be useful to assist in subtly altering the mind and thinning the veil to the unseen. If one is working with certain planetary bodies and or entities they may feel inclined to incorporate an incense or fragrance associated with such. Referring to the ancient *Greek Magical Papyri (PGM)*[4], a list for the main planetary bodies and their designated fragrances could be as follows:

Saturn	Styrax – Likely the resin of Liquidambar orientalis (oriental sweetgum/storax balsam), noted for its heavy, fragrant quality.
Jupiter	Malabathron (μαλάβαθρον) – Leaves of Cinnamomum tamala (Indian bay leaf/tejpat); aromatic, spicy leaf used in ancient trade.
Mars	Costus (κόστος) – Root of Saussurea lappa (costus root/snow lotus); pungent, earthy, medicinal scent.
Sun	Frankincense (λίβανον) – Resin of Boswellia species; the classic solar incense, bright and purifying.
Venus	Indian Nard / Spikenard (νάρδος Ἰνδικός) – Nardostachys jatamansi; rich, musky, floral-earthly oil/resin.
Mercury	Cassia (κασσία) – Bark of Cinnamomum cassia (Chinese cinnamon); sharp, warm, spicy.
Moon	Myrrh (σμύρνα) – Resin of Commiphora myrrha; bitter, balsamic, deeply lunar and shadowy.

If choosing to work with different entities - such as the archangels - a related substitution may be made utilizing the above table. For example, Archangel Michael has often been equated with the Sun, Raphael with Mercury, and Gabriel with the Moon. For Uriel - as often relating to Earth - a similar connection to Saturn may be implemented. Oftentimes, due to price and or accessibility limitations, a fragrance with similar qualities has been substituted. A quick list likely containing more accessible suffumigation alternatives for some of the planetary bodies - much in line with Aleister Crowley's system detailed in his 'Liber 777'[5] - that may be employed are: Saturn ~ Myrrh; Jupiter ~ Cedar; Mars ~ Dragons Blood; Sun ~ Frankincense; Venus ~ Sandalwood; Mercury ~

Cinnamon; Moon ~ Jasmine; and Earth ~ Patchouli.

In like manner, a crystal or a combination of crystals present may also be beneficial, especially upon them having been cleansed in living/running water and or saltwater in addition to being charged under the sun or moonlight. Amethyst has frequently been associated with opening the 'third eye' and moonstone could be fitting for the deck as well. Some citrine might serve to further cleanse and quartz could be appropriate for directing intention. Something heavy such as obsidian or magnetite, moreover, may act as a grounding anchor so that one does not entirely float away during the endeavor.

A final recommendation for this chapter could be regarding the breath. As my teacher has taught, breathing is one of the first experiences that one partakes in upon birth as well as being one of the last acts engaged in prior to crossing the great divide. By learning to control the breath one may learn to control the mind. From self healing via an infusion of oxygen into the system to inducing states of lucidity or euphoria, breathwork has been an integral aspect within many traditions - such as Yoga, the Martial Arts, and Sufism to name but a few. For the purposes of this discourse we may limit the purview to a single though effective technique termed 'box breathing.'

While seated in an upright posture with muscles relaxed, you may do your best to tune out discursive thoughts and focus solely on your breath. First, breathe deeply into your diaphragm so that your lower abdomen expands - ideally your chest should not expand until the very end of the breath - counting slowly to four as you do so. Once your lungs are full, hold the breath for another slow four count. Then, slowly release the breath as you count to four. Lastly, while no breath remains, hold for another count of four. You may then repeat the cycle if desired and time permits. One may employ this technique for a single cycle, for four cycles, or even to begin an extended meditation session where one is no longer even counting, merely listening to the breath; flowing in and out like the tides of the ocean. With practice, this simple technique may serve to quiet the 'monkey mind' as well as to potentially facilitate entrance into the theta brainwave state. There - similar to the mindstate of having just woken from sleep - one may become more in tune with the liminal space beyond the veil of ordinary perception. By connecting to this astral, lunar realm, your receptivity to the messages being transmitted through the tarot may increase dramatically.

BANISHING AND PROTECTION

In conjunction with setting the stage, one may also choose to perform a protection and or banishing type ritual. Considering a more traditional Western esoteric approach, a banishing ritual such as the Lesser Banishing Ritual of the Pentagram (LBRP) may be employed. A simple template type version of the LBRP adapted from Israel Regardie's *The Golden Dawn*[6] could be as follows: Stand facing east with your legs about shoulder width apart and your arms at your sides. You may begin by performing the Qabalistic Cross. Raising your right arm and using your right forefinger - or a wand, consecrated dagger, or similar instrument - touch a spot in the air just above your head that can be visualized as divine light and then bring your light imbued finger down to touch the 'third eye' area by the middle of your forehead while vocalizing in a rhythmic vibratory manner: "Ateh..." Next, bring your finger downward and touch your abdomen approximately two inches below your navel - though some traditions may suggest touching your groin - and intone: "Malkuth..." Next, move your finger to touch your right shoulder - some practitioners reverse the shoulders - and say: "Ve-Geburah..." Then to the left shoulder vibrating: "Ve-Gedulah..." Next, you can bring both hands to your solar plexus area to connect them palm to palm with fingers extended together pointing upwards in a prayer-like fashion and recite: "Le-Olam... Amen..."

After having performed the Qabalistic Cross, you may extend your right arm and index finger - or instrument - out in front of you to an area approximately level with the outside of your left hip - this point on the pentagram can symbolize earth. For simplicity here we may start at this point for each direction - east, south, west, and north - though one may incorporate different starting points and direction of travel for each pentagram depending upon elemental correspondence and intent - such as banishing, invocation, etc.. Then, with your arm and finger still extended out in front of your left hip, keep your arm extended though proceed to move it to a point out in front of your forehead area, then down to a point level with the outside of your right hip, then to an area in front of your left shoulder followed by a point before your right shoulder before returning it the starting point in front of your left hip to complete the pentagram - five pointed star. While drawing the pentagrams you may visualize the lines as composed of shimmering blue flames. Next, draw your finger in part of the way to your chest and then extend it back out straight in front of you towards the center of the pentagram and vibrate: "Yod.. Heh... Vav... Heh..."

Next, with your arm still extended and moving in unison with your body as it shifts directions, adjust your feet and body position so that you are facing south. Here you may draw the same flaming pentagram though when extending your finger out towards the center of the pentagram you may intone: "Adonai..." Next, continue the procedure to the west and use the name: "Ehyeh (Eh-heh-yeh)..." Lastly, the name used in the north can be: "AGLA (Agala)..." With the index finger still extended one can turn again to the east to complete the 360° circle connecting all four pentagrams. Finally, shift your index finger to your lips like you are motioning for someone to 'shush' in order to give the 'sign of silence.'

 Afterwards, return your arm to your side and announce: "Before me Raphael; behind me,

Gabriel; on my right hand, Michael; on my left hand, Uriel. For about me flames the pentagram and in the Column shines the six-rayed star." One may then complete the banishing ritual by performing another Qabilistic Cross.

If partaking in various types of ritual feels awkward and or doesn't seem to produce immediate 'results,' please do not let yourself be discouraged. One may adjust certain elements if felt drawn to do so; however, as with most arts, repetition leads to mastery. According to the formula of: 'Obedience, Divergence, Separation;' one may initially follow the prescribed structure more verbatim early on; then, after a certain level of mastery has been achieved, they may start experimenting more and more. Finally, after the material has been thoroughly integrated, one may incorporate the information learned and then make it their own. Additionally, working with a mentor may serve to accelerate your progress and potentially assist in avoiding certain pitfalls, though that doesn't necessarily mean one should avoid practicing on their own beforehand. As the old saying goes, 'when the student is ready, the teacher will appear.'

Regarding spiritual teachers, choosing to learn from those with more experience may serve to be very beneficial, yet being mindful of their intentions may be even more so. My teacher put it something like: "it's good to have an open heart, though not a fool's heart." The teacher can be like a guide that has traveled the path before. Nevertheless, each must travel their own path and the landscape may not always remain static. If ever questioning which route to take, one may find that listening to their intuition can serve as an excellent compass, especially when able to sufficiently quiet the mind.

If coming from a religious background and or the LBRP provided above feels beyond your comfort zone, there are alternatives that may produce similar results. From a more Christian perspective we may reference a masterpiece work entitled '*Meditations on the Tarot*' by an anonymous author. There, the author provides the following directional banishing: 'Make the sign of the Cross towards the north, south, east, and west, each time reciting the first two verses of Psalm 68: "Let God arise, let his enemies be scattered; let those who hate him flee before him! As smoke is driven away, so drive them away; as wax melts before fire, let the wicked perish before God!"'[7]

Lastly, from an Islamicate perspective, a Quranic verse recitation for protection recognizing Allah's dominion over all, could be Ayat al-Kursi Quran 2:255 (Pickthall): "Allah! There is no Allah save Him, the Alive, the Eternal. Neither slumber nor sleep overtaketh Him. Unto Him belongeth whatsoever is in the heavens and whatsoever is in the earth. Who is he that intercedeth with Him save by His leave? He knoweth that which is in front of them and that which is behind them, while they encompass nothing of His knowledge save what He will. His throne includeth the heavens and the earth, and He is never weary of preserving them. He is the Sublime, the Tremendous."

Prior to a reading one may also appeal to a divine source or sources for knowledge, wisdom, illumination, etc.. In the vein of Western esoteric tradition, one may supplicate to Hermes-Thoth-Mercury who has long been affiliated with the tarot. For this purpose one may recite an invocation from the *Greek Magical Papyri* (PGM): "Hermes, lord of the cosmos, who are in the heart, O wheel of Selene, spherical and square, First founder of the words of speech, Who plead for justice, O all-subduer, unsubdued, O mantle-wearer, golden-sandaled, Charioteer of the airy course beneath the chthonic abyss, Eye of Helios, first author of full-voiced speech! Lord of the world, in the heart, You who bring forth the light, who are in the light, Who make the torch shine, who grant glory, Who are the eye of the world, who lead souls, Who descend into Tartarus, who rise again, Who come forth from the fire, who are in the fire, Who are in the water, who are in the air, Who are in the earth, who are everywhere— Come to me, O blessed one, come quickly, Be present at this sacred rite, And grant that this dream-oracle come to pass for me."[4]

Similarly, through a Judeo-Christian lens, one can recite from scripture such as the following verse from the Book of Daniel (KJV): "Daniel answered and said, Blessed be the name of God for ever and ever: for wisdom and might are his: And he changeth the times and the seasons: he removeth kings, and setteth up kings: he giveth wisdom unto the wise, and knowledge to them that know understanding: He revealeth the deep and secret things: he knoweth what is in the darkness, and the light dwelleth with him." Another similar verse from the Judeo-Christian realm could be Jeremiah 33:3 (KJV): "Call unto me, and I will answer thee, and shew thee great and mighty things, which thou knowest not."

For a more or less equivalent version from the Islamicate tradition, a Quranic verse that one could recite for such a purpose is Ayat an-Nur Quran

24:35 (Pickthall): "Allah is the Light of the heavens and the earth. The similitude of His light is as a niche wherein is a lamp. The lamp is in a glass. The glass is as it were a shining star. (This lamp is) kindled from a blessed tree, an olive neither of the East nor of the West, whose oil would almost glow forth (of itself) though no fire touched it. Light upon light. Allah guideth unto His light whom He will. And Allah speaketh to mankind in allegories, for Allah is Knower of all things."

SPREADS

There exist numerous card spreads that practitioners may utilize to suit their specific preference, inquiry type, and time frame. For simplicity and brevity's sake, we may limit our explanation here to only a few relatively quick methods of laying out the cards for a reading. The spreads discussed in this section may not be entirely original though sometimes methods that are popular are so for a reason.

With the stage set, one may shuffle the cards and pose the question/s for inquiry. In regards to shuffling, some like to do a traditional full riffle shuffle possibly finishing with an aesthetic waterfall if card size and durability permit - although, even if it is a heavy card stock with a game style finish the deck may wear out much more quickly this way than via other methods. Alternatively, especially for larger decks, one can do a corner only dovetail shuffle by slowly releasing one corner of the cards - or along one side - from your thumbs and letting the stack of cards in each hand alternately fall into place together on the table. When all the cards have been interlaced at the corner you may push the piles together into one. You could also gather the entire pile into one hand and then begin letting several cards at a time fall into the other in semi regular increments as a method of shuffling. An alternative could be spreading the cards out in a buffet-like pile on the table and then mixing them all up before gathering them together - or even choosing the card/s while the deck is splayed out. Cutting the deck into two or three piles then stacking the piles on top of each other after shuffling has also been popular. Furthermore, many readers suggest asking the querent to do the deck cutting - if reading for another person. If you prefer not to let others imbue your cards with their energy, however, that could be understandable. In this regard you could also have a deck intended for performing readings for others and another for personal use.

Regarding the query, Susan T. Chang may have said something analogous to ~ "rather than asking for a direct foretelling of the future, instead one may like to ask what to contemplate regarding the potential future outcome in question." For example, instead of asking if you will get the job tomorrow, you could instead posit the query as a question regarding what factors should be considered to improve the chances of landing the job and or what might be helpful to contemplate if it fell through. Moreover, from a psychological perspective, the reading's results for this type of question may open the querent up to thought processes that may prove useful and had not yet been considered.

At last, with the deck shuffled and the question posed, one may proceed to lay the card spread out. A bit of a side note that we can address here is that different practitioners may have variant preferences as to how they turn over the cards. One may choose to turn the cards over directly from the top of the deck and lay them out face up, particularly for single card readings. Be that as it may, for many other spreads it has been recommended to lay the cards out face down prior to turning them over. Also, when turning over the face down card, tradition has often been to reveal the card from the top to the bottom. Whatever the case, if you feel called to pursue alternate methods please do not feel compelled to restrict yourself solely to convention.

For a simple query, especially when constrained for time, a basic one card reading may suffice. Furthermore, one may choose to draw an additional card or cards for further elaboration if not fully satisfied with the answer given by the sole card. Please reference the General Card Interpretations chapter for further information regarding interpreting the card/s drawn.

Please note that the one card draw could also be an ideal method for the purposes of seeking guidance from the divine for meditation and or contemplation purposes in lieu of strictly divinatory reasons. In such a case, the card could be drawn and placed in view while in a comfortable position. There are a variety of techniques that may be employed though some might include dwelling on the different aspects of the card - visual elements, attributions, corresponding scripture, etc. - and considering their relevance, cohesion, and potential application to circumstances. The card could be gazed upon and absorbed, then, with the eyes closed, reflected upon while recalling specific card elements. Additionally, one may imagine oneself being transported inside of the scene displayed on the card, immersing oneself in the surroundings, the archetypal motifs, and or interacting with the props, characters, and or principals. Instead of choosing a card to employ these techniques with at random, one could also choose a specific card that they feel drawn to and or could follow a prescribed order. For instance, you could begin with the Fool card and embark on your own Fool's/Hero's Journey while exploring each of the cards - particularly from the major arcana - for a period of time and processing what insight and or lessons each card may reveal.

A similar simple spread, read in like fashion, could be a three card spread where three cards are laid out and interpreted in a past, present, and future context regarding the inquiry. If English is one's primary language where text is traditionally read from left to right, then that may be the direction one might like to read the past, present, and future order of the cards in. However, in both Hebrew and Arabic, the text is read from right to left so one may prefer to read the cards in that order.

Lastly, for a more in depth though possibly more time consuming reading the 'Eight Directions of Life and Death Spread' - whose name we adapted from a Goju Ryu term found in Roy Kamen's book 'Karate: Beneath The Surface'[8] - could be implemented. After deciding on a subject of inquiry, one may choose the subject card at random and place it in the center of the reading area or may instead deliberately choose the subject card as a representation of the query. For instance, if the subject of the inquiry refers to a person, one may sort through the deck and choose a card that befits their personage - many readers have used one of the court cards in reference to particular individuals. After selecting the subject card - and possibly shuffling the deck if needed - the remaining cards may be laid out face down surrounding the central subject card in a shape reminiscent of a compass, with the North (N), South (S), East (E), and West (W) cards spaced slightly further away from the central card than the four cards placed in the diagonal directions; ie Northeast (NE), Southeast (SE), Southwest (SW), and Northwest (NW). For the sake of simplicity in this example we may refer to the different cards according to their directional position and can read the past to the future from left to right - though one may reverse that order if desired. With the cards laid out face down surrounding the central card - which can be turned face up if not already - we can start with the card in the west and turn that card over. The W card may represent some of the past circumstances and or situations that have contributed to the current position of the subject. Next, we can turn over the E card representative of a possible future direction that the subject is heading if the subject does not alter their current trajectory. Then, we can turn over the N card which can represent what the subject may aspire to and or helps to elevate them. After that, we may turn over the S card to determine factors that may either provide foundational support or possibly even drag the subject down - the difference depending upon context and card interplay. Next, the NW card may be turned over which can elucidate the current state of the Society of which the subject is a part. Then, turning over the NE card may inform as to the state of Nature around the individual. Proceeding to turn over the SE card may divulge the state of the Individual, as in their 'self' or Ego. Lastly, one may turn over the SW card where they may reveal the state of the Soul of the subject. The reader may then formulate the findings into a narrative surrounding the subject, ideally ushering in clarity regarding circumstances and or rousing themes for further contemplation. There are a multitude of diverse spreads with a wide variety of applications though we have included a few here which the reader may find useful.

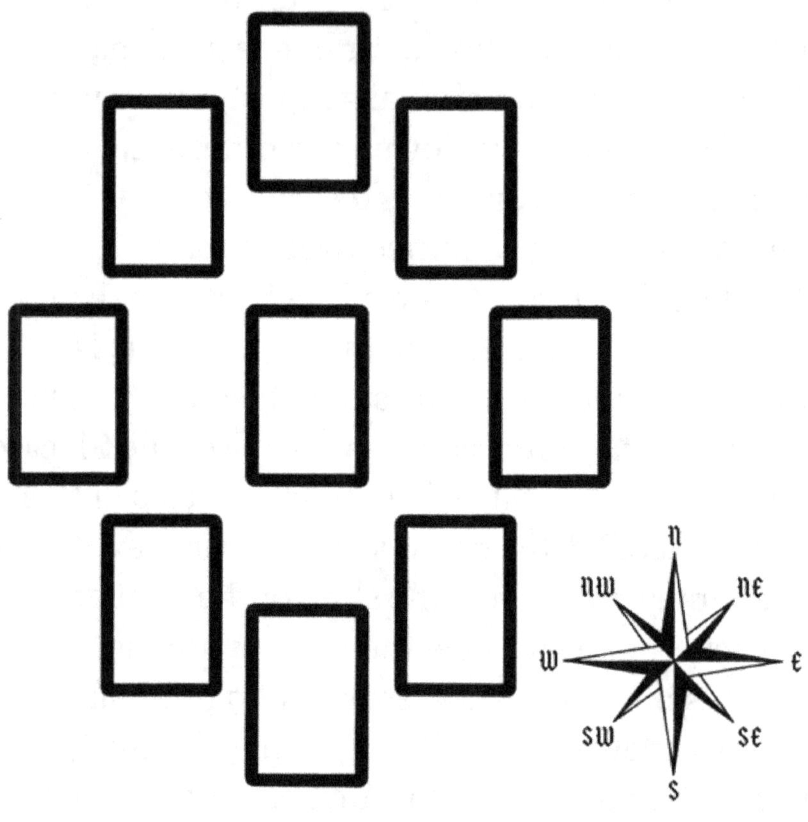

GENERAL CARD INTERPRETATIONS

Although there may be as many interpretations for each tarot card as there are card readers - if not more - one may find it useful to have a quick reference guide for card meanings accessible. Some readers prefer an intuitive approach based upon their feelings, intuition, and or visual cues for card meanings and interplay whereas others may prefer a more methodical approach based upon traditional correspondences. Oftentimes, intuitive readers in particular may struggle with interpreting cards in the minor arcana. However, if one incorporates the use of correspondences in such a case the interplay of meanings per card may expound dramatically.

We quite relished how Mel Meleen and Susan T Chang described on the Fortune's Wheelhouse Podcast[9] the various card categories. Their description was something akin to ~ "Each of the major arcana are like a word, each of the pip cards are like a sentence, and the court cards are like paragraphs." To elaborate further upon said statement, the major arcana often capture a single archetypal character, symbol, and or theme;

whereas the pip cards often reference several of the majors - based upon their number, their sign attribution, as well as their planetary association.

For example, the Two of Wands has the number two so it adopts that numerical association with the High Priestess card. The Two of Wands is attributed with the zodiacal sign of Aries so also relates to the Emperor card. Additionally, the planetary attribution of the Two of Wands is Mars so the Tower card may also be applied. Hence, the Two of Wands pip card alone may encompass the High Priestess, the Emperor, and the Tower cards from the major arcana. What's more is that the Two of Wand's Hermetic title is the 'Lord of Dominion' - shortened to just 'Dominion' in the People of the Night Tarot as Aleister Crowley did in his Thoth deck - which may further expand upon the card's meaning. For even greater depth, the Two of Wands in the People of the Night Tarot has also been linked to the Lunar Mansion 'al-Sharatan.' For further properties regarding the Lunar Mansions please reference the table in the Lunar Mansions chapter.

Finally, the Kings, Queens, and Princes from the court cards each span three of the pip cards thereby encompassing the associations of all three . The Princesses and Aces contain even more information by engulfing nine of the pip cards in addition to their seasonal and elemental attributions. For details as to which cards fall where, please reference the wheel in the Astrological Wheel chapter.

Although The People of the Night Tarot has incorporated attributions familiar to many western tarot enthusiasts, the correspondences drawn from the Islamicate tradition may provide an even greater breadth of information to draw upon. If perchance one finds an overabundance of information when considering all of the above, they may decide to limit their readings to only some of the cues associated with each card. Additionally, if choosing to limit the amount of information to interpret from, many prefer to avoid reading card reversals as separate from the standard meanings. Alternatively, if you do feel inclined to assess reversed cards as being distinct, you could view them as potential energy blocks or the vices to the standard position's virtue. We have included a possible meaning for reversals in addition to optional upright card connotations. Although there might not be any one 'correct' way to read the tarot, one may discover the following general card meanings, divine names, and associated verse/s helpful, especially as a quick reference during live readings or even for meditative and contemplative purposes.

THE MAJOR ARCANA

PEOPLE OF THE NIGHT ALTAR CARD

Manuscript folio 84a, Shams al-Ma'arif al-Kubrā, ca. 16th c., Beinecke Rare Book & Manuscript Library, Yale University (MS 32304220)

While not constituting one of the 78 cards proper that make up the major and minor arcana, we have included as a 'Joker' card an excerpt page from the the *Shams al-Ma'arif (the Sun of Knowledge)* grimoire attributed to the infamous mystic and scholar Ahmad al-Būnī. The page portrayed was where the phrase ~ "The People of the Night are given in the darkness what is not given in the light"[1] was derived and from which The People of the Night Tarot drew its name. The page may also feature a magic square related to acquiring hidden knowledge and protection, particularly during night rituals. This card can be utilized as an altar plaque to be laid flat or propped up on the table or altar so as to set the tone for the reading, meditation, and or contemplation.

0 ~ THE FOOL / THE CHILD

Qualities: Awe, Wonder, Potential

Inversion: Ignorance, Naivety, Reckless

Verse/s: ~ Matthew 18:1-5 (KJV) At the same time came the disciples unto Jesus, saying, Who is the greatest in the kingdom of heaven? And Jesus called a little child unto him, and set him in the midst of them, And said, Verily I say unto you, Except ye be converted, and become as little children, ye shall not enter into the kingdom of heaven. Whosoever therefore shall humble himself as this little child, the same is greatest in the kingdom of heaven. And whoso shall receive one such little child in my name receiveth me

~ Sahih al-Bukhari 7017: The Prophet Muhammad (ﷺ) said: "Every child is born in a state of fitrah (the pure natural disposition toward Allah), then his parents make him a Jew, or a Christian, or a Magian."[10]

I ~ THE MAGICIAN / THE WITCH

Qualities: Strategy, Intelligence, Agency
Inversion: Improvisation, Instinct, Providence
Verse/s: ~ 1 Samuel 28:6-7 (KJV) And when Saul enquired of the LORD, the LORD answered him not, neither by dreams, nor by Urim, nor by prophets. Then said Saul unto his servants, Seek me a woman that hath a familiar spirit, that I may go to her, and enquire of her. And his servants said to him, Behold, there is a woman that hath a familiar spirit at Endor.

~ Surah Al-A'raf 7:113–122 (Pickthall) And the wizards came to Pharaoh, saying: Surely there will be a reward for us if we are the winners? He answered: Yes, and ye shall be of those brought near (to the throne). They said: O Moses! Either throw (thy staff) or let us be the first throwers. He answered: Throw! And when they threw, they cast a spell upon the people's eyes, and awed them, and they had a mighty spell. And We inspired Moses (saying): Throw thy staff! And lo! it swallowed up their lying show. Thus was the Truth vindicated and that which they were doing was made vain.

Thus were they vanquished there, and they were made to come low. And the wizards fell prostrate, Crying: We believe in the Lord of the Worlds, The Lord of Moses and Aaron.

II ~ THE HIGH PRIESTESS

Qualities: Mysteries, Insight, Depth
Inversion: Revelation, Immanence, Spontaneity
Verse/s: ~ Gospel of Mary (Berlin Codex) Peter said to Mary, "Sister, we know that the Savior loved you more than the rest of women. Tell us the words of the Savior which you remember which you know, but we do not, nor have we heard them." Mary answered and said, "What is hidden from you I will proclaim to you."[11]

~ Sahih al-Bukhari 3: Narrated 'Aisha (the mother of the faithful believers): ...Then Allah's Messenger (ﷺ) returned with the Inspiration and with his heart beating severely. Then he went to Khadija bint Khuwailid and said, "Cover me! Cover me!" They covered him till his fear was over and after that he told her everything that had happened and said, "I fear that something may happen to me." Khadija replied, "Never! By Allah, Allah will never disgrace you...[12]

III ~ THE EMPRESS / THE QUEEN

Qualities: Attentive, Patient, Endearing
Inversion: Preoccupied, Restless, Reserved
Verse/s: ~ Jeremiah 7:18 (KJV) The children gather wood, and the fathers kindle the fire, and the women knead their dough, to make cakes to the queen of heaven...
~ Pre-Islamic Quraysh tawaf chant (invocation during circumambulation of the Kaaba; also referred to as the Satanic Verses / Gharaniq incident linked to Surah An-Najm 53:19–23): "By al-Lat and al-'Uzza, And Manat, the third, the other; Verily they are the exalted gharaniq (high-flying cranes/lofty ones), Whose intercession is to be hoped for / sought / approved."[13]
~ Hymn to Ishtar (Old Babylonian Akkadian, ca.

65

1800–1600 BCE) "Sing of the goddess, most awe-inspiring of goddesses! Let the mistress of peoples be praised, the greatest of the Igigi-gods! Sing of Ishtar, most awe-inspiring of goddesses! Let the queen of women, the greatest of the Igigi, be revered. Ishtar among the gods—extraordinary is her station. Respected is her word; it is supreme over them. She is their queen; they continually cause her commands to be executed. All of them bow down to her. They receive her light before her. Women and men indeed revere her."[14]

IV ~ THE EMPEROR / THE SHOGUN

Qualities: Leadership, Role Model, Guardian
Inversion: Autonomy, Iconoclast, Antagonist
Verse/s: ~ Psalm 110:1 (KJV) The LORD said unto my Lord, Sit thou at my right hand, until I make thine enemies thy footstool.
~ Surah Al-Anfal 6:61 (Pickthall) He is the Omnipotent over His slaves. He sendeth guardians over you until, when death cometh unto one of you,

Our messengers receive him, and they neglect not.

V ~ THE HIEROPHANT / THE SHEIKH

Qualities: Righteousness, Initiation, Guidance
Inversion: Complex, Gestation, Appraisal
Verse/s: ~ Hebrews 6:19–20 (KJV) Which hope we have as an anchor of the soul, both sure and stedfast, and which entereth into that within the veil; Whither the forerunner is for us entered, even Jesus, made an high priest for ever after the order of Melchisedec.

~ Surah Al-Kahf 18:65–66 (Pickthall) Then found they one of Our slaves, unto whom We had given mercy from Us, and had taught him from Our presence a knowledge. Moses said unto him: May I follow thee, to the end that thou mayst teach me right conduct of that which thou hast been taught?

VI ~ THE LOVERS

Qualities: Conjunction, Passion, Devotion
Inversion: Transgressive, Antinomian, Promiscuity
Verse/s: ~ Song of Solomon 2:1–3 (KJV) I am the rose of Sharon, and the lily of the valleys. As the lily among thorns, so is my love among the daughters. As the apple tree among the trees of the wood, so is my beloved among the sons. I sat down under his shadow with great delight, and his fruit was sweet to my taste.

~ Surah Ar-Rum 30:21 (Pickthall) And among His Signs is this, that He created for you mates from among yourselves, that ye may dwell in tranquillity with them, and He has put love and mercy between your (hearts): verily in that are Signs for those who reflect.

VII ~ THE CHARIOT

Qualities: Endurance, Orchestration, Victory
Inversion: Evanescence, Improvisation, Tactical Egress
Verse/s: ~ Psalm 89:2 (KJV) For I have said, Mercy shall be built up for ever: thy faithfulness shalt thou establish in the very heavens.
~ Sahih al-Bukhari 4281 Narrated by Abdullah bin Mughaffal: "I saw Allah's Messenger (ﷺ) on the day of the Conquest of Mecca over his she-camel, reciting Surat-al-Fath (The Victory) in a vibrant quivering tone."[15]

VIII ~ STRENGTH

Qualities: Power, Confidence, Potency
Inversion: Corruption, Controlling, Coercion
Verse/s: ~ Philippians 4:13 (KJV) I can do all things through Christ which strengtheneth me.
~ Surah Sad 38:36-38 (Pickthall) So We made the wind subservient unto him, setting fair by his command whithersoever he intended. And the unruly, every builder and diver (of the jinn), And others linked together in fetters.

IX ~ THE HERMIT / THE SAGE

Qualities: Knowledge, Wisdom, Counsel
Inversion: Clandestine, Enigma, Misdirection
Verse/s: ~ Proverbs 11:14 (KJV) Where no counsel is, the people fall: but in the multitude of counsellors there is safety.
~ Surah Al-Alaq 96:1-5

(Pickthall) Read: In the name of thy Lord Who createth, Createth man from a clot. Read: And thy Lord is the Most Bounteous, Who teacheth by the pen, Teacheth man that which he knew not.

X ~ THE WHEEL OF FORTUNE

Qualities: Change, Fluctuation, Seasons
Inversion: Instability, Chaos, Usurpation
Verse/s: ~ Job 38:31–32 (KJV) Canst thou bind the sweet influences of Pleiades, or loose the bands of Orion? Canst thou bring forth Mazzaroth in his season? or canst thou guide Arcturus with his sons?

~ Surah Ya-Sin 36:37–40 (Pickthall) And a portent for them is the night. We withdraw therefrom the day, and lo! they are in darkness. And the sun runneth on unto a resting-place for him. That is the measuring of the Mighty, the Wise. And for the moon We have appointed mansions till she return like an old shrivelled palm-leaf. It is not for the sun to overtake the moon, nor for the night to outstrip the day. They float each in an orbit.

XI ~ JUSTICE

Qualities: Impartiality, Objectivity, Atonement
Inversion: Discrimination, Obstruction, Blackmail
Verse/s: ~ Luke 6:38 (KJV) Give, and it shall be given unto you; good measure, pressed down, and shaken together, and running over, shall men give into your bosom. For with the same measure that ye mete withal it shall be measured to you again.

~ Surah Al-Qari'ah 101:6–9 (Pickthall) Then, as for him whose deeds weigh heavy (on the scale), He will live a pleasant life. But as for him whose deeds weigh light, his mother will be the Abyss. And what will explain unto thee what the Abyss is? A raging fire!

XII ~ THE HANGED MAN

Qualities: Contemplation, Meditation, Numinous
Inversion: Adrift, Ungrounded, Desanctification
Verse/s: ~ Matthew 19:12 (KJV) For there are some eunuchs, which were so born from their mother's womb: and there are some eunuchs, which were made eunuchs of men: and there be eunuchs, which have made themselves eunuchs for the kingdom of heaven. He that is able to receive it, let him receive it.

~ Sahih al-Bukhari 1904 The Prophet (ﷺ) said: "Every deed of the son of Adam is multiplied — a good deed is multiplied tenfold up to seven hundred times — except fasting, for it is for Me alone and I shall reward it. He gives up his desires and his food for My sake."[16]

XIII ~ DEATH

Qualities: Fermentation, Transformation, Evolution
Inversion: Fixation, Immutable, Regression
Verse/s: ~ Ephesians 5:14 (KJV) Wherefore he saith, Awake thou that sleepest, and arise from the dead, and Christ shall give thee light.
~ Surah az-Zumar 39:42 (Pickthall) Allah receiveth (men's) souls at the time of their death, and those that die not (He receiveth) during their sleep. He keepeth those (souls) for which He hath ordained death and sendeth the others back for a term appointed. Lo! herein verily are portents for people who reflect.

XIV ~ TEMPERANCE

Qualities: Balance, Discipline, Forging

Inversion: Capricious, Unfettered, Forbearing

Verse/s: ~ Song of Solomon 5:1 (KJV) I am come into my garden, my sister, my spouse: I have gathered my myrrh with my spice; I have eaten my honeycomb with my honey; I have drunk my wine with my milk: eat, O friends; drink, yea, drink abundantly, O beloved.

~ Sahih al-Bukhari 6114 Narrated Abu Hurairah: The Messenger of Allah ﷺ said: "Anger comes from the devil, and the devil was created from fire, and water extinguishes fire, so when one of you becomes angry, let him perform wudu (ablution)."[17]

XV ~ THE DEVIL

Qualities: Fear, Bondage, Idolatry
Inversion: Ambition, Drive, Motivation
Verse/s: ~ Matthew 6:22–23 (KJV) The light of the body is the eye: if therefore thine eye be single, thy whole body shall be full of light. But if thine eye be evil, thy whole body shall be full of darkness. If therefore the light that is in thee be darkness, how great is that darkness!

~ Sahih Muslim 1599 Narrated an-Nuʿmān ibn Bashīr: The Messenger of Allah ﷺ said: "That which is lawful is clear and that which is unlawful is clear, and between the two of them are doubtful matters about which many people do not know. Thus he who avoids doubtful matters clears himself in regard to his religion and his honour, but he who falls into doubtful matters falls into that which is unlawful, like the shepherd who pastures around a sanctuary, all but grazing therein. Truly, every king has a sanctuary, and truly Allah's sanctuary is His prohibitions. Truly, in the body there is a morsel of flesh which, if it is sound, the whole body is sound and which, if it is diseased, the whole body is diseased. Truly, it is the heart."[18]

XVI ~ THE TOWER / THE VOLCANO

Qualities: Calcination, Destabilization, Fragmentation
Inversion: Sublimation, Energizing, Purification
Verse/s: ~ Isaiah 14:12–15 (KJV) How art thou fallen from heaven, O Lucifer, son of the morning! how art thou cut down to the ground, which didst weaken the nations! For thou hast said in thine heart, I will ascend into heaven, I will exalt my throne above the stars of God: I will sit also upon the mount of the congregation, in the sides of the north: I will ascend above the heights of the clouds; I will be like the most High. Yet thou shalt be brought down to hell, to the sides of the pit.

~ Sahih Muslim 91a (Book 1, Hadith 164) Narrated Abdullah ibn Mas'ud: The Messenger of Allah (ﷺ) said: He who has in his heart the weight of a mustard seed of pride shall not enter Paradise...[19]

XVII ~ THE STAR

Qualities: Peace, Quietude, Hope
Inversion: Ferocity, Hyperphantasia, Imperative
Verse/s: ~ Colossians 1:26–27 (KJV) Even the mystery which hath been hid from ages and from generations, but now is made manifest to his saints: To whom God would make known what is the riches of the glory of this mystery among the Gentiles; which is Christ in you, the hope of glory.
~ Narration attributed to the Prophet Muhammad ﷺ (via Abu Hurairah): "One of Bilqis's parents was from among the jinn."[20]

XVIII ~ THE MOON

Qualities: Dreamtime, Hypnotic, Phosphorecence
Inversion: Hallucination, Derealization, Void
Verse/s: ~ Acts 2:20–21 (KJV) The sun shall be turned into darkness, and the moon into blood, before that great and notable day of the Lord come: And it shall come to pass, that whosoever shall call on the name of the Lord shall be saved.

~ Sahih al-Bukhari 297 Narrated `Aisha: The Prophet (ﷺ) used to lean on my lap and recite Qur'an while I was in menses.[21]

XIX ~ THE SUN

Qualities: Truth, Life, Radiance
Inversion: Riddle, Quintessence, Twilight
Verse/s: ~ Luke 12:2–3 (KJV)
For there is nothing covered, that shall not be revealed; neither hid, that shall not be known. Therefore whatsoever ye have spoken in darkness shall be heard in the light; and that which ye have spoken in the ear in closets shall be proclaimed upon the housetops.
~ Surah Al-Haqqah 69:18 (Pickthall) On that day ye will be exposed; not a secret of yours will be hidden.

XX ~ JUDGEMENT

Qualities: Rebirth, Forgiveness, Apocalypse
Inversion: Catharsis, Ablution, Nascence
Verse/s: ~ Mark 5:39–42 (KJV) And when he was come in, he saith unto them, Why make ye this ado, and weep? the damsel is not dead, but sleepeth. And they laughed him to scorn. But when he had put them all out, he taketh the father and the mother of the damsel, and them that were with him, and entereth in where the damsel was lying. And he took the damsel by the hand, and said unto her, Talitha cumi; which is, being interpreted, Damsel, I say unto thee, arise. And straightway the damsel arose, and walked; for she was of the age of twelve years. And they were astonished with a great astonishment.

~ Sahih al-Bukhari 6324 Upon waking, the Prophet ﷺ would say: "Al-hamdu lillahil-ladhi ahyana ba'da ma amatana wa ilayhin-nushur." (All praise is due to Allah Who has given us life after causing us to die [sleep], and unto Him is the resurrection.)[22]

XXI ~ THE WORLD

Qualities: Coagulation, Attainment, Completion
Inversion: Translucence, Serendipity, Inception
Verse/s: ~ Luke 4:5–8 (KJV) And the devil, taking him up into an high mountain, shewed unto him all the kingdoms of the world in a moment of time. And the devil said unto him, All this power will I give thee, and the glory of them: for that is delivered unto me; and to whomsoever I will I give it. If thou therefore wilt worship me, all shall be thine. And Jesus answered and said unto him, Get thee behind me, Satan: for it is written, Thou shalt worship the Lord thy God, and him only shalt thou serve.

~ Sunan al-Tirmidhi 2346 (Hasan) The Messenger of Allah ﷺ said: "Whoever among you wakes up secure in his property, healthy in his body, and has his food for the day, it is as if the whole world has been gathered for him."[23]

THE MINOR ARCANA

WANDS ~ FIRE △

KING OF WANDS

Qualities: Voracious, Authority, Stalwart
Inversion: Surly, Tyrannical, Fickle
Divine Name: ~ القاهر / الْقَهَّارُ ~ Al-Qahhār ~ The Subduer
Verse/s: ~ Exodus 3:2 (KJV) And the angel of the LORD appeared unto him in a flame of fire out of the midst of a bush: and he looked, and, behold, the bush burned with fire, and the bush was not consumed.

~ Surah Ta-Ha 20:111 (Pickthall) And faces humble themselves before the Living, the Self-subsistent. And he who beareth (a burden of) wrongdoing is indeed a failure (on that day).

QUEEN OF WANDS

Qualities: Counterpoise, Nourishment, Integration
Inversion: Instability, Depletion, Division
Divine Name: اللطيف ~ Al-Laṭīf ~ The Subtle
Verse/s: ~ Song of Solomon 8:6–7 (KJV) Set me as a seal upon thine heart, as a seal upon thine arm: for love is strong as death; jealousy is cruel as the grave: the coals thereof are coals of fire, which hath a most vehement flame. Many waters cannot quench love, neither can the floods drown it...

~ Surah Al-An'am 6:103 (Pickthall) Vision comprehendeth Him not, but He comprehendeth (all) vision. He is the Subtile, the Aware.

PRINCE OF WANDS

Qualities: Brilliance, Confidence, Ardent
Inversion: Gloom, Apprehension, Shrouded
Divine Name: النور ~ An-Nūr ~ The Light
Verse/s: ~ Ezekiel 1:13 (KJV) As for the likeness of the living creatures, their appearance was like burning coals of fire, and like the appearance of lamps: it went up and down among the living creatures; and the fire was bright, and out of the fire went forth lightning.

~ Surah An-Nur 24:35 (Pickthall) Allah is the Light of the heavens and the earth. The likeness of His light is as a niche wherein is a lamp. The lamp is in a glass. The glass is as it were a shining star. (This lamp is) kindled from a blessed tree, an olive neither of the East nor of the West, whose oil would almost glow forth (of itself) though no fire touched it. Light upon light. Allah guideth unto His light whom He will. And Allah speaketh to mankind in allegories, for Allah is Knower of all things.

PRINCESS OF WANDS

Qualities: Actualization, Aspiration, Rubedo
Inversion: Rebellion, Disinclination, Nigredo
Divine Name: القادر ~ Al-Qādir ~ The All-Powerful
Verse/s: ~ Exodus 13:21 (KJV) And the LORD went before them by day in a pillar of a cloud, to lead them the way; and by night in a pillar of fire, to give them light; to go by day and night.
~ Surah Ya-Sin 36:82 (Pickthall) His command, when He intendeth a thing, is only that He saith unto it: Be! and it is.

10 OF WANDS

Qualities: Binding, Submission, Smothering

Inversion: Breaking the Chains, Reversal, Liberation

Verse/s: ~ Sahih al-Bukhari 519 Narrated `Aisha: It is not good that you people have made us (women) equal to dogs and donkeys. No doubt I saw Allah's Messenger (ﷺ) praying while I used to lie between him and the Qibla and when he wanted to prostrate, he pushed my legs and I withdrew them.[24]

~ Samurai maxim: They told the Warrior: 'A storm is coming.' The Warrior replied: 'I am the storm.'

9 OF WANDS

Qualities: Infusion, Attrition, Foundation
Inversion: Dissemination, Circumvention, Capstone
Verse/s: ~ Isaiah 40:31 (KJV) But they that wait upon the LORD shall renew their strength; they shall mount up with wings as eagles; they shall run, and not be weary; and they shall walk, and not faint.

~ Surah Al-Imran 3:159-160 (Pickthall) ...And when thou art resolved, then put thy trust in Allah. Lo! Allah loveth those who put their trust (in Him). If Allah is your helper none can overcome you...

8 OF WANDS

Qualities: Synergy, Momentum, Ploy
Inversion: Friction, Encumbrance, Stagnation
Verse/s: ~ Ecclesiastes 9:11 (KJV) I returned, and saw under the sun, that the race is not to the swift, nor the battle to the strong, neither yet bread to the wise, nor yet riches to men of understanding, nor yet favour to men of skill; but time and chance happeneth to them all.

~ Sun Tzu: Swift as the wind. Quiet as the forest. Conquer like the fire. Steady as the mountain.[25]

7 OF WANDS

Qualities: Heroism, Chivalry, Bravery

Inversion: Timidity, Barbarism, Retreat

Verse/s: ~ Joshua 1:9 (KJV) Have not I commanded thee? Be strong and of a good courage; be not afraid, neither be thou dismayed: for the LORD thy God is with thee whithersoever thou goest.

~ Balian of Ibelin, Kingdom of Heaven (2005 film) "Be without fear in the face of your enemies. Be brave and upright that God may love thee. Speak the truth always, even if it leads to your death. Safeguard the helpless and do no wrong."[26]

6 OF WANDS

Qualities: Recognition, Achievement, Vitality
Inversion: Obscurity, Mundaneness, Lethargy
Verse/s: ~ 2 Timothy 4:5-7 (KJV) But watch thou in all things, endure afflictions, do the work of an evangelist, make full proof of thy ministry. For I am now ready to be offered, and the time of my departure is at hand. I have fought a good fight, I have finished my course, I have kept the faith: ~ If (Rudyard Kipling) If you can keep your head when all about you, Are losing theirs and blaming it on you, If you can trust yourself when all men doubt you, But make allowance for their doubting too; If you can wait and not be tired by waiting, Or being lied about, don't deal in lies, Or being hated, don't give way to hating, And yet don't look too good, nor talk too wise; If you can fill the unforgiving minute, With sixty seconds' worth of distance run, Yours is the Earth and everything that's in it, And—which is more—you'll be a Man, my son![27]

5 OF WANDS

Qualities: Friction, Tribulation, Grit

Inversion: Evasion, Exultation, Lassitude

Verse/s: ~ Matthew 3:11 (KJV) I indeed baptize you with water unto repentance: but he that cometh after me is mightier than I, whose shoes I am not worthy to bear: he shall baptize you with the Holy Ghost, and with fire.

~ Roosevelt, Theodore: "It is not the critic who counts; not the man who points out how the strong man stumbles, or where the doer of deeds could have done them better. The credit belongs to the man who is actually in the arena, whose face is marred by dust and sweat and blood; who strives valiantly; who errs, who comes short again and again, because there is no effort without error and shortcoming; but who does actually strive to do the deeds; who knows great enthusiasms, the great devotions; who spends himself in a worthy cause; who at the best knows in the end the triumph of high achievement, and who at the worst, if he fails, at least fails while daring greatly, so that his place shall never be with those cold and timid souls who neither know victory nor defeat."[28]

4 OF WANDS

Qualities: Culmination, Consummation, Conjunctio
Inversion: Nadir, Cessation, Separatio
Verse/s: ~ John 19:28-30 (KJV) After this, Jesus knowing that all things were now accomplished, that the scripture might be fulfilled, saith, I thirst. Now there was set a vessel full of vinegar: and they filled a spunge with vinegar, and put it upon hyssop, and put it to his mouth. When Jesus therefore had received the vinegar, he said, It is finished: and he bowed his head, and gave up the ghost.

~ Surah Al-Ma'idah 5:3 (Pickthall) This day have I perfected your religion for you and completed My favour unto you, and have chosen for you as religion al-Islam.

3 OF WANDS

Qualities: Radiance, Benevolence, Nobility
Inversion: Opaque, Indignation, Banality
Verse/s: ~ 2 Peter 1:4-7 (KJV) Whereby are given unto us exceeding great and precious promises: that by these ye might be partakers of the divine nature, having escaped the corruption that is in the world through lust. And beside this, giving all diligence, add to your faith virtue; and to virtue knowledge; And to knowledge temperance; and to temperance patience; and to patience godliness; And to godliness brotherly kindness; and to brotherly kindness charity.

~ Sahih Muslim 199 Abu Huraira reported: The Messenger of Allah ﷺ said, "Every prophet has a supplication that is answered and has hastened his supplication. I will delay my supplication as intercession for my nation on the Day of Resurrection. It is granted, if Allah wills, to whoever dies in my nation not associating anything with Allah."[29]

2 OF WANDS

Qualities: Sovereignty, Magnanimity, Self-Effacing

Inversion: Servitude, Parsimony, Vainglory

Verse/s: ~ Philippians 2:8-11 (KJV) And being found in fashion as a man, he humbled himself, and became obedient unto death, even the death of the cross. Wherefore God also hath highly exalted him, and given him a name which is above every name: That at the name of Jesus every knee should bow, of things in heaven, and things in earth, and things under the earth; And that every tongue should confess that Jesus Christ is Lord, to the glory of God the Father.

~ Surah Ar-Ra'd 13:15 (Pickthall) And unto Allah prostrateth whosoever is in the heavens and the earth, willingly or unwillingly, as do their shadows in the morning and the evening hours.

ACE OF WANDS

Qualities: Sacred Masculine, Will, Penetrative

Inversion: Despot, Determinism, Disinterested

Angel: מִיכָאֵל ~ Michael ~ ميكائيل ~ Mīkāʾīl

Verse/s: ~ Acts 2:3–4 (KJV) And there appeared unto them cloven tongues like as of fire, and it sat upon each of them. And they were all filled with the Holy Ghost, and began to speak with other tongues, as the Spirit gave them utterance.

~ Surah Ar-Rum 30:48 (Pickthall) Allah is He Who sendeth the winds so that they raise clouds, and spreadeth them along the sky as He will, and breaketh them, so that thou seest the rain come forth from within them. And when He maketh it to fall on whom He will of His bondmen, lo! they rejoice;

CUPS ~ WATER ∇

KING OF CUPS

Qualities: Genial, Appeasement, Ardency
Inversion: Belligerent, Resistance, Malaise
Divine Name: الرحمن ~
Ar-Raḥmān ~ The Most Merciful
Verse/s: ~ Isaiah 43:2 (KJV) When thou passest through the waters, I will be with thee; and through the rivers, they shall not overflow thee: when thou walkest through the fire, thou shalt not be burned; neither shall the flame kindle upon thee.

~ Surah Ar-Rahman 55:1-2 (Pickthall) The Beneficent Hath made known the Qur'an. He created man.

QUEEN OF CUPS

Qualities: Sensitive, Fluid, Emotive

Inversion: Sappy, Unstable, Vindictive

Divine Name: ~ الستير / الستار ~ As-Sattār ~ The Coverer of Sins

Verse/s: ~ Psalm 42:7 (KJV) Deep calleth unto deep at the noise of thy waterspouts: all thy waves and thy billows are gone over me.

~ Surah Ghafir 40:19 (Pickthall) He knoweth the treachery of the eye and that which the bosoms hide.

PRINCE OF CUPS

Qualities: Holistic, Authentic, Rumination
Inversion: Reductionist, Machiavellian, Transference
Divine Name: الودود ~
Al-Wadūd ~ The Affectionate
Verse/s: ~ Psalm 104:3 (KJV) Who layeth the beams of his chambers in the waters: who maketh the clouds his chariot: who walketh upon the wings of the wind.

~ Surah Hud 11:90 (Pickthall) And ask forgiveness of your Lord and then repent unto Him. Lo! my Lord is Merciful, Loving.

PRINCESS OF CUPS

Qualities: Adept, Nurturing, Empathic
Inversion: Dormant, Callous, Antagonistic
Divine Name: الغفور ~
Al-Ghafūr ~ The Forgiving
Verse/s: ~ Genesis 2:6 (KJV) But there went up a mist from the earth, and watered the whole face of the ground.
~ Surah Az-Zumar 39:53 (Pickthall) Say: O My slaves who have been prodigal to their own hurt! Despair not of the mercy of Allah, Who forgiveth all sins. Lo! He is the Forgiving, the Merciful.

10 OF CUPS

Qualities: Gorged, Gluttony, Prodigal
Inversion: Famished, Abstinence, Stewardship
Verse/s: ~ Proverbs 25:16
Hast thou found honey? eat so much as is sufficient for thee, lest thou be filled therewith, and vomit it.
~ Surah Al-An'am 6:141
(Pickthall) And it is He Who produceth gardens trellised and untrellised, and the palm-tree, and crops of different flavour, and the olive and the pomegranate, like and unlike. Eat ye of the fruit thereof when it fruiteth, and pay the due thereof upon the day of its harvest, and be not prodigal. Lo! He loveth not the prodigals.

9 OF CUPS

Qualities: Nirvana, Ecstasty, New Jerusalem

Inversion: Pandemonium, Oblivion, Perdition

Verse/s: ~ Philippians 4:8–9 (KJV) Finally, brethren, whatsoever things are true, whatsoever things are honest, whatsoever things are just, whatsoever things are pure, whatsoever things are lovely, whatsoever things are of good report; if there be any virtue, and if there be any praise, think on these things.

~ Sunan Ibn Majah 238 Narrated Sahl bin Sa'd: The Messenger of Allah ﷺ said: "This goodness contains many treasures, and for those there are keys. So glad tidings to the one whom Allah makes a key to good and a lock for evil (مفتاحًا للخير مغلاقًا للشر), and woe to the one whom Allah makes a key to evil and a lock to good."[30]

8 OF CUPS

Qualities: Sloth, Stasis, Laurelled Ease
Inversion: Zealotry, Dynamism, Unremitting
Verse/s: ~ 2 Thessalonians 3:10-12 (KJV) For even when we were with you, this we commanded you, that if any would not work, neither should he eat. For we hear that there are some which walk among you disorderly, working not at all, but are busybodies. Now them that are such we command and exhort by our Lord Jesus Christ, that with quietness they work, and eat their own bread.

~ Sahih al-Bukhari 2072 Narrated Al-Miqdam bin Ma'dikarib: The Prophet (ﷺ) said, "Nobody has ever eaten a better meal than that which one has earned by working with one's own hands. The Prophet of Allah, David (عليه السلام), used to eat from the earnings of his own hands."[31]

7 OF CUPS

Qualities: Venus in Furs, Superfluity, Venery
Inversion: Demure, Asceticism, Chastity
Verse/s: ~ Surah Al-Ḥadīd 57:20 (Pickthall) Know that the life of the world is but a play and idle pastime, and pageantry and boasting among you, and rivalry in respect of wealth and children; as the likeness of vegetation after rain, whereof the growth is pleasing to the husbandman, but afterward it withereth and thou seest it turning yellow, then becometh straw. And in the Hereafter is grievous punishment and (also) forgiveness from Allah and good pleasure, whereas the life of the world is but matter of illusion.

~ Navy SEAL saying: "Never lose sight of the shoreline."[32]

6 OF CUPS

Qualities: Communion, Contentment, Consummation
Inversion: Sacrilege, Covetousness, Lechery
Verse/s: ~ Isaiah 22:12-14 (KJV) And in that day did the Lord GOD of hosts call to weeping, and to mourning, and to baldness, and to girding with sackcloth: And behold joy and gladness, slaying oxen, and killing sheep, eating flesh, and drinking wine: let us eat and drink; for to morrow we shall die. And it was revealed in mine ears by the LORD of hosts, Surely this iniquity shall not be purged from you till ye die, saith the Lord GOD of hosts.

~ Surah Ar-Rahman 55:66-71 (Pickthall) Wherein are two abundant springs. Which is it, of the favours of your Lord, that ye deny? Wherein is fruit, the date-palm and pomegranate. Which is it, of the favours of your Lord, that ye deny? Therein (gardens) will be fair (wives) good and beautiful; Which is it, of the favours of your Lord, that ye deny?

5 OF CUPS

Qualities: Discord, Gilded Cage, Crucible
Inversion: Reconciliation, Cornucopia, Quenching
Verse/s: ~ 2 Corinthians 12:7 (KJV) And lest I should be exalted above measure through the abundance of the revelations, there was given to me a thorn in the flesh, the messenger of Satan to buffet me, lest I should be exalted above measure.

~ Surah Al-Ankabut 29:2-3 (Pickthall) Do men imagine that they will be left (at ease) because they say, We believe, and will not be tested with fitnah? Lo! We tested those who were before you. Thus Allah knoweth those of you who are sincere, and knoweth those who feign.

4 OF CUPS

Qualities: Boredom, Jaded, Transitory
Inversion: Flow-State, Vibrant, Enduring
Verse/s: ~ Matthew 6:19-21 (KJV) Lay not up for yourselves treasures upon earth, where moth and rust doth corrupt, and where thieves break through and steal: But lay up for yourselves treasures in heaven, where neither moth nor rust doth corrupt, and where thieves do not break through nor steal: For where your treasure is, there will your heart be also.

~ Sahih Muslim 1048a Narrated Anas: Anas reported Allah's Messenger (ﷺ) as saying: If the son of Adam were to possess two valleys of riches, he would long for the third one. And the stomach of the son of Adam is not filled but with dust. And Allah returns to him who repents.[33]

3 OF CUPS

Qualities: Affluence, Splendor, Harem

Inversion: Squalor, Austerity, Monogamy

Verse/s: ~ Matthew 12:34–35 (KJV) O generation of vipers, how can ye, being evil, speak good things? for out of the abundance of the heart the mouth speaketh. A good man out of the good treasure of the heart bringeth forth good things: and an evil man out of the evil treasure bringeth forth evil things. ~ Sunan at-Tirmidhī 2000 Narrated Abu Hurairah: The Messenger of Allah ﷺ said: "The most sacred part of the animal is its tongue and its heart. And the most evil part of the animal is its tongue and its heart."[34]

2 OF CUPS

Qualities: Enshined, Adoration, Blending
Inversion: Veiled, Libertine, Divestment
Verse/s: ~ Genesis 2:24 (KJV) Therefore shall a man leave his father and his mother, and shall cleave unto his wife: and they shall be one flesh.
~ Sunan al-Tirmidhi 3880 Narrated 'Aishah: that Jibril came to the Prophet (ﷺ) with her image upon a piece of green silk cloth, and he said: 'This is your wife in the world, and in the Hereafter.'[35]

ACE OF CUPS

Qualities: Sacred Feminine, Emotion, Receptive
Inversion: Jezebel, Affectless, Guarded
Angel: גַּבְרִיאֵל ~ Gabriel ~ جبريل ~ Jibrīl
Verse/s: ~ Luke 1:28–30 (KJV) And the angel came in unto her, and said, Hail, thou that art highly favoured, the

Lord is with thee: blessed art thou among women. And when she saw him, she was troubled at his saying, and cast in her mind what manner of salutation this should be. And the angel said unto her, Fear not, Mary: for thou hast found favour with God.

~ Surah Al-Baqarah 2:97 (Pickthall) Say (O Muhammad, to mankind): Who is an enemy to Gabriel! for he it is who hath revealed (this Scripture) to thy heart by Allah's leave, confirming that which was (revealed) before it, and a guidance and glad tidings for believers;

SWORDS ~ AIR △

KING OF SWORDS

Qualities: Passionate, Maverick, Agile
Inversion: Apathetic, Square, Obtuse
Divine Name: الحق ~ Al-Ḥaqq ~ The Truth
Verse/s: ~ Ezekiel 1:27 (KJV) And I saw as the colour of amber, as the appearance of fire round about within it, from the appearance of his loins even upward, and from the appearance of his loins even downward, I saw as it were the appearance of fire, and it had brightness round about.

~ Surah Al-Hajj 22:6 (Pickthall) That is because Allah, He is the Truth and because He quickeneth the dead, and because He is Able to do all things;

QUEEN OF SWORDS

Qualities: Calculating, Adaptable, Insightful
Inversion: Unfiltered, Rigid, Facade
Divine Name: الكافي ~ Al-Kāfī ~ The Sufficient
Verse/s: ~ Proverbs 2:3–6 (KJV) Yea, if thou criest after knowledge, and liftest up thy voice for understanding; If thou seekest her as silver, and searchest for her as for hid treasures; Then shalt thou understand the fear of the LORD, and find the knowledge of God. For the LORD giveth wisdom: out of his mouth cometh knowledge and understanding.

~ Surah Ta-Ha 20:7 (Pickthall) And if thou speakest aloud, then lo! He knoweth the secret (thought) and (that which is yet) more hidden.

PRINCE OF SWORDS

Qualities: Cerebral, Eloquent, Quick

Inversion: Mindless, Incoherent, Somnolent

Divine Name: المتكلم ~ Al-Mutakallim ~ The Speaker

Verse/s: ~ Job 37:21 (KJV) And now men see not the bright light which is in the clouds: but the wind passeth, and cleanseth them.

~ Surah Ar-Rahman 55:3-4 (Pickthall) He created man. He taught him utterance.

PRINCESS OF SWORDS

Qualities: Tempest, Tenebrous, Paradox
Inversion: Tranquil, Placid, Congruity
Divine Name: المتكبّر ~ Al-Mutakabbir ~ The Supreme
Verse/s: ~ Proverbs 15:3 (KJV) The eyes of the LORD are in every place, beholding the evil and the good.

~ Surah Al-Hashr 59:23 (Pickthall) He is Allah, than Whom there is no other Allah, the Sovereign Lord, the Holy One, Peace, the Keeper of Faith, the Guardian, the Majestic, the Compeller, the Superb. Glorified be Allah from all that they ascribe as partner (unto Him).

10 OF SWORDS

Qualities: Debasement, Degradation, Desecration
Inversion: Exaltation, Elevation, Sanctification
Verse/s: ~ Daniel 4:30-33 (KJV) The king spake, and said, Is not this great Babylon, that I have built for the house of the kingdom by the might of my power, and for the honour of my majesty? While the word was in the king's mouth, there fell a voice from heaven, saying, O king Nebuchadnezzar, to thee it is spoken; The kingdom is departed from thee. And they shall drive thee from men, and thy dwelling shall be with the beasts of the field: they shall make thee to eat grass as oxen, and seven times shall pass over thee, until thou know that the most High ruleth in the kingdom of men, and giveth it to whomsoever he will. The same hour was the thing fulfilled upon Nebuchadnezzar: and he was driven from men, and did eat grass as oxen, and his body was wet with the dew of heaven, till his hairs were grown like eagles' feathers, and his nails like birds' claws.

~ Surah An-Nisa 4:145-146 (Pickthall) Lo! the

hypocrites (will be) in the lowest deep of the Fire, and thou wilt find no helper for them; Save those who repent and amend and hold fast to Allah and make their religion pure for Allah (only). Those are with the believers. And Allah will bestow on the believers a mighty reward.

9 OF SWORDS

Qualities: Malice, Turmoil, Enmity
Inversion: Faith, Equanimity, Symbiosis
Verse/s: ~ Matthew 8:28-32 (KJV) And when he was come to the other side into the country of the Gergesenes, there met him two possessed with devils, coming out of the tombs, exceeding fierce, so that no man might pass by that way. And, behold, they cried out, saying, What have we to do with thee, Jesus, thou Son of God? art thou come hither to torment us before the time? And there was a good way off from them an herd of many swine feeding. So the devils besought him, saying, If thou

cast us out, suffer us to go away into the herd of swine. And he said unto them, Go. And when they were come out, they went into the herd of swine: and, behold, the whole herd of swine ran violently down a steep place into the sea, and perished in the waters.

~ Musnad Ahmad, vol. 4 (pp. 170-173) Narrated Ya'la ibn Murrah: "I witnessed three things from the Messenger of Allah ﷺ that no one witnessed before me or after me. [...] We were traveling when we passed by some water. A woman came with her son and said: 'O Messenger of Allah, this son of mine is afflicted (by the jinn/Shaytan), and he gets fits/madness many times a day.' The Prophet ﷺ said: 'Bring him to me.' So she brought him close, and the Prophet ﷺ placed him between himself and the saddle. He opened the boy's mouth, spat into it three times, and said: 'In the name of Allah, I am the slave of Allah, get out, O enemy of Allah!' (Bismillah, ana 'abdullah, ikhruj 'aduww Allah!). He repeated this, then returned the boy to her and said: 'Meet us here on our return and tell us how he is.' We continued, and on our way back, we found the woman in the same place with three sheep. She said: 'By the One who sent you with the truth, we have seen nothing wrong in him since then.' The Prophet ﷺ said: 'Take one for yourself and leave the rest with her.'"[36]

8 OF SWORDS

Qualities: Deflection, Impediment, Hindrance
Inversion: Candor, Facilitation, Impetus
Verse/s: ~ Psalm 91:9-12 (KJV) Because thou hast made the LORD, which is my refuge, even the most High, thy habitation; There shall no evil befall thee, neither shall any plague come nigh thy dwelling. For he shall give his angels charge over thee, to keep thee in all thy ways. They shall bear thee up in their hands, lest thou dash thy foot against a stone.

~ Surah Aal-E-Imran 3:54-55 (Pickthall) And they (the disbelievers) schemed, and Allah schemed (against them): and Allah is the best of schemers. (And remember) when Allah said: O Jesus! Lo! I am gathering thee and causing thee to ascend unto Me, and am cleansing thee of those who disbelieve and am setting those who follow thee above those who disbelieve until the Day of Resurrection. Then unto Me ye will (all) return, and I shall judge between you as to that wherein ye used to differ.

7 OF SWORDS

Qualities: Fantasy, Utopia, Phantasmagoria
Inversion: Manifest, Substantive, Clarity
Verse/s: ~ Proverbs 26:27 (KJV) Whoso diggeth a pit shall fall therein: and he that rolleth a stone, it will return upon him.
~ Surah An-Nur 24:39 (Pickthall) As for those who disbelieve, their deeds are as a mirage in a desert. The thirsty supposeth it to be water till, when he cometh unto it, he findeth it naught, and he findeth Allah there, Who payeth him his due; and Allah is swift at reckoning.

6 OF SWORDS

Qualities: Alchemy, Tradecraft, Methodology
Inversion: Irreverance, Hubris, Ad Hoc
Verse/s: ~ Surah Al-Baqarah 2:102 (Pickthall) And they followed that which the devils falsely recited during the reign of Solomon. Solomon disbelieved not, but the devils disbelieved, teaching mankind sorcery and that which was revealed to the two angels in Babylon, Harut and Marut. Nor did they teach anyone until they had said: We are only a temptation, therefore disbelieve not. Yet they learned from them that by which they cause division between man and wife; but they injure thereby no-one save by Allah's leave. And they learn that which harmeth them and profiteth them not; and surely they do know that he who trafficketh therein will have no happy portion in the Hereafter; and surely evil is the price for which they sell their souls, if they but knew.

~ 1 Enoch 8:1-3 (R.H. Charles translation) And Azâzêl taught men to make swords, and knives, and shields, and breastplates, and made known to them the metals of the earth and the art of working them, and bracelets, and ornaments, and the use of antimony, and the beautifying of the eyelids, and all kinds of costly stones, and all colouring tinctures. And there arose much godlessness, and they committed fornication, and they were led astray, and became corrupt in all their ways. Semjâzâ taught enchantments, and root-cuttings, Armârôs the resolving of enchantments, Barâqîjâl (taught) astrology, Kôkabêl the constellations, Ezêqêêl the knowledge of the clouds, Araqiêl the signs of the earth, Shamsiêl the signs of the sun, and Sariêl the course of the moon. And as men perished, they cried, and their cry went up to heaven...[37]

5 OF SWORDS

Qualities: Depersonalization, Dissonance, Subjugation
Inversion: Integration, Consonance, Liberation
Verse/s: ~ Surah Aal-E-Imran 3:139-141 (Pickthall) Faint not nor grieve, for ye will overcome them if ye are (indeed) believers. If ye have received a blow, the

(disbelieving) people have received a blow the like thereof. These are days which We alternate among mankind that Allah may know those who believe and may choose witnesses from among you; and Allah loveth not wrong-doers; And that He may purge those who believe and may wipe out the disbelievers.

~ Japanese Proverb: Nana korobi ya oki / Fall down seven times, stand up eight.

~ Litany Against Fear (Dune, Frank Herbert) I must not fear. Fear is the mind-killer. Fear is the little-death that brings total obliteration. I will face my fear. I will permit it to pass over me and through me. And when it has gone past I will turn the inner eye to see its path. Where the fear has gone there will be nothing. Only I will remain.[38]

4 OF SWORDS

Qualities: Reconciliation, Compromise, Accord
Inversion: Schism, Absolutism, Deadlock
Verse/s: ~ Genesis 33:1-4 (KJV) And Jacob lifted up his eyes, and looked, and, behold, Esau came, and with him four hundred men. And he divided the children unto Leah, and unto Rachel, and unto the two handmaids. And he put the handmaids and their children foremost, and Leah and her children after, and Rachel and Joseph hindermost. And he passed over before them, and bowed himself to the ground seven times, until he came near to his brother. And Esau ran to meet him, and embraced him, and fell on his neck, and kissed him: and they wept.

~ Surah Ash-Shura 42:40 (Pickthall) The recompense of an evil is an evil like thereof. But whosoever pardons and makes reconciliation, his reward is due from Allah. Verily, He likes not wrong-doers.

3 OF SWORDS

Qualities: Lamentation, Release, Acceptance
Inversion: Revelry, Suppression, Denial
Verse/s: ~ John 11:33-35 (KJV) When Jesus therefore saw her weeping, and the Jews also weeping which came with her, he groaned in the spirit, and was troubled, And said, Where have ye laid him? They said unto him, Lord, come and see. Jesus wept.

~ Sahih al-Bukhari 1284 Narrated Usamah bin Zaid: We were with Allah's Messenger (ﷺ) when a message came from one of his daughters, calling him to her son who was at his last breath. The Prophet (ﷺ) went, and we went with him. He took the child in his lap, and his eyes started shedding tears. Abdur-Rahman bin Auf said, "O Allah's Messenger! Even you are weeping!" He said, "O Ibn Auf, this is mercy which Allah has lodged in the hearts of His slaves, and Allah is merciful only to those of His slaves who are merciful (to others)."[39]

2 OF SWORDS

Qualities: Serenity, Mildness, Contentment

Inversion: Agitation, Harshness, Perturbed

Verse/s: ~ Philippians 4:6-7 (KJV) Be careful for nothing; but in every thing by prayer and supplication with thanksgiving let your requests be made known unto God.

And the peace of God, which passeth all understanding, shall keep your hearts and minds through Christ Jesus.

~ Surah Ar-Ra'd 13:28 (Pickthall) Those who believe and whose hearts find rest in the remembrance of Allah. Verily in the remembrance of Allah do hearts find rest!

ACE OF SWORDS

Qualities: Mentalism, Psyche, Thought

Inversion: Materialism, Soma, Sensation

Angel: עֲזַרְאֵל ~ Azrael ~ عزرائیل ~ Azrā'īl

Verse/s: ~ Hebrews 4:12 (KJV) For the word of God is quick, and powerful, and sharper than any twoedged sword, piercing even to the dividing asunder of soul and spirit, and of the joints and marrow, and is a discerner of the thoughts and intents of the heart.

~ Surah As-Sajdah 32:11 (Pickthall) Say: The angel of death, who hath charge concerning you, will take you. Then unto your Lord ye will be returned.

PENTACLES ~ EARTH ▽

KING OF PENTACLES

Qualities: Ascetism, Chastity, Modest
Inversion: Hedonist, Debauchery, Pompous
Divine Name: القوي ~
Al-Qawiyy ~ The Strong
Verse/s: ~ Daniel 3:25 (KJV) He answered and said, Lo, I see four men loose, walking in the midst of the fire, and they have no hurt; and the form of the fourth is like the Son of God.

~ Surah Al-Hajj 22:40 (Pickthall) Those who have been driven from their homes unjustly because they said: Our Lord is Allah - for had it not been for Allah's repelling some men by means of others, cloisters and churches and oratories and mosques, wherein the name of Allah is oft mentioned, would assuredly have been pulled down. Verily Allah helpeth one who helpeth Him. Lo! Allah is Strong, Almighty -

QUEEN OF PENTACLES

Qualities: Bountiful, Lush, Imaginative
Inversion: Deficient, Arid, Banal
Divine Name: الكريم ~ Al-Karīm ~ The Generous
Verse/s: ~ Psalm 65:9–10 (KJV) Thou visitest the earth, and waterest it: thou greatly enrichest it with the river of God, which is full of water: thou preparest them corn, when thou hast so provided for it. Thou waterest the ridges thereof abundantly: thou settlest the furrows thereof: thou makest it soft with showers: thou blessest the springing thereof.

~ Surah Al-Infitar 82:6-7 (Pickthall) O man! What hath made thee careless concerning thy Lord, the Bountiful, Who created thee, then fashioned, then proportioned thee?

PRINCE OF PENTACLES

Qualities: Pragmatic, Industrious, Innovative
Inversion: Idealist, Listless, Uninventive
Divine Name: الرزاق ~
Ar-Razzāq ~ The Provider
Verse/s: ~ Proverbs 14:4 (KJV) Where no oxen are, the crib is clean: but much increase is by the strength of the ox.

~ Surah Adh-Dhariyat 51:58 (Pickthall) Lo! Allah! He it is that giveth livelihood, the Lord of unbreakable might.

PRINCESS OF PENTACLES

Qualities: Grounded, Artisanship, Durability
Inversion: Ungrounded, Wild, Unstable
Divine Name: الحي ~ Al-Ḥayy ~ The Ever-Living
Verse/s: ~ Psalm 65:11 (KJV) Thou crownest the year with thy goodness; and thy paths drop fatness.

~ Surah Al-Baqarah 2:255 (Pickthall – Ayat al-Kursi) Allah! There is no god save Him, the Alive, the Eternal. Neither slumber nor sleep overtaketh Him. Unto Him belongeth whatsoever is in the heavens and whatsoever is in the earth. Who is he that intercedeth with Him save by His leave? He knoweth that which is in front of them and that which is behind them, while they encompass nothing of His knowledge save what He will. His throne includeth the heavens and the earth, and He is never weary of preserving them. He is the Sublime, the Tremendous.

10 OF PENTACLES

Qualities: Gratitude, Prosperity, Opulence
Inversion: Ingratitude, Poverty, Frugality
Verse/s: ~ Matthew 16:24-26 (KJV) Then said Jesus unto his disciples, If any man will come after me, let him deny himself, and take up his cross, and follow me. For whosoever will save his life shall lose it:

and whosoever will lose his life for my sake shall find it. For what is a man profited, if he shall gain the whole world, and lose his own soul? or what shall a man give in exchange for his soul?
~ Surah Ibrahim 14:7 (Pickthall) And when your Lord proclaimed: If ye give thanks, I will give you more; but if ye are thankless, lo! My punishment is dire.

9 OF PENTACLES

Qualities: Increase, Reward, Profit
Inversion: Detachment, Punishment, Fine
Verse/s: ~ Acts 10:34 (KJV) Then Peter opened his mouth, and said, Of a truth I perceive that God is no respecter of persons: But in every nation he that feareth him, and worketh righteousness, is accepted with him.
~ Sunan Abi Dawud 3851 Narrated Abu Ayyub al-Ansari: When the Messenger of Allah (ﷺ) ate or drank, he said: "Praise be to Allah Who has given food and drink and made it easy to swallow, and provided an exit for it."[40]

~ Gondorian prophecy (J.R.R. Tolkien, The Return of the King) "Renewed shall be blade that was broken: The crownless again shall be king."[41]

8 OF PENTACLES

Qualities: Humility, Mindfullness, Discernment
Inversion: Arrogance, Neglectful, Indiscriminate
Verse/s: ~ Proverbs 20:5 (KJV) Counsel in the heart of man is like deep water; but a man of understanding will draw it out.
~ Sahih Muslim 2729 Narrated Abu Hurairah: The Messenger of Allah (ﷺ) said: "Look at those who are below you and do not look at those who are above you, for it is more suitable that you should not consider as less the blessing of Allah to you."[42]

7 OF PENTACLES

Qualities: Discontent, Stalemate, Submission
Inversion: Contententment, Headway, Counteroffensive
Verse/s: ~ Isaiah 53:4-5 (KJV) Surely he hath borne our griefs, and carried our sorrows: yet we did esteem him stricken, smitten of God, and afflicted. But he was wounded for our transgressions, he was bruised for our iniquities: the chastisement of our peace was upon him; and with his stripes we are healed.

~ Apollo 13 (1995 film): "Failure is not an option."[43]

~ Plutarch (from Moralia, "Sayings of Spartan Women," Mor. 241): A Spartan mother, handing her son his shield as he went off to war, said: "Either with this or upon this." (Come back with your shield — or on it.)[44]

6 OF PENTACLES

Qualities: Ascend, Fruition, Compensation
Inversion: Descend, Fruitless, Debt
Verse/s: ~ 1 Corinthians 15:54-57 (KJV) So when this corruptible shall have put on incorruption, and this mortal shall have put on immortality, then shall be brought to pass the saying that is written, Death is swallowed up in victory. O death, where is thy sting? O grave, where is thy victory? The sting of death is sin; and the strength of sin is the law. But thanks be to God, which giveth us the victory through our Lord Jesus Christ.

~ Surah Al-Baqarah 2:1-7 (Pickthall) Alif. Lam. Mim. This is the Scripture whereof there is no doubt, a guidance unto those who ward off (evil). Who believe in the Unseen, and establish worship, and spend of that We have bestowed on them; And who believe in that which is revealed unto thee (Muhammad) and that which was revealed before thee, and are certain of the Hereafter. These depend on guidance from their Lord. These are the successful. As for the disbelievers, whether thou warn them or warn them not it is all alike for them;

they believe not. Allah hath sealed their hearing and their hearts, and on their eyes there is a covering. Theirs will be an awful doom.

5 OF PENTACLES

Qualities: Pretense, Logistics, Analyze

Inversion: Carefree, Chaos, Shirk

Verse/s: ~ Matthew 6:25-34 (KJV) Therefore I say unto you, Take no thought for your life, what ye shall eat, or what ye shall drink; nor yet for your body, what ye shall put on. Is not the life more than meat, and the body than raiment? Behold the fowls of the air: for they sow not, neither do they reap, nor gather into barns; yet your heavenly Father feedeth them. Are ye not much better than they? Which of you by taking thought can add one cubit unto his stature? And why take ye thought for raiment? Consider the lilies of the field, how they grow; they toil not, neither do they spin: And yet I say unto you, That even Solomon in all his glory was not arrayed like one of these. Wherefore, if God so clothe the grass of the field, which to day is, and to morrow is cast into the oven, shall he not much more clothe you, O ye of little faith? Therefore take no thought, saying, What shall we eat? or, What shall we drink? or, Wherewithal shall we be clothed? (For after all these things do the Gentiles seek:) for your heavenly Father knoweth that ye have need of all these things. But seek ye first the kingdom of God, and his righteousness; and all these things shall be added unto you. Take therefore no thought for the morrow: for the morrow shall take thought for the things of itself. Sufficient unto the day is the evil thereof.

~ Sahih al-Bukhari 6064 Narrated Abu Huraira: The Prophet ﷺ said, "Beware of suspicion, for suspicion is the worst of false tales; and do not look for the others' faults and do not spy, and do not be jealous of one another, and do not desert (cut your relation with) one another, and do not hate one another; and O Allah's worshipers! Be brothers (as Allah has ordered you!)"[45]

4 OF PENTACLES

Qualities: Prowess, Authority, Majesty
Inversion: Inept, Subordinate, Inconsequential
Verse/s: ~ Isaiah 34:13-15 (KJV) And thorns shall come up in her palaces, nettles and brambles in the fortresses thereof: and it shall be an habitation of dragons, and a court for owls. The wild beasts of the desert shall also meet with the wild beasts of the island, and the satyr shall cry to his fellow; the screech owl also shall rest there, and find for herself a place of rest. There shall the great owl make her nest, and lay, and hatch, and gather under her shadow: there shall the vultures also be gathered, every one with her mate.

~ Confucius (The Analects of Kongzi / Confucius) In ruling, be just; in speech, be truthful; in action, observe the proper timing.[46]

3 OF PENTACLES

Qualities: Authenticity, Congruency, Productivity
Inversion: Hypocrisy, Incongruency, Unproductive
Verse/s: ~ James 2:18-20 (KJV) Yea, a man may say, Thou hast faith, and I have works: shew me thy faith without thy works, and I will shew thee my faith by my works. Thou believest that there is one God; thou doest well: the devils also believe, and tremble. But wilt thou know, O vain man, that faith without works is dead?

~ Sahih al-Bukhari 6496 Umar ibn al-Khattab reported: The Messenger of Allah (ﷺ) said: "Actions are judged by intentions, and every person will have what they intended."[47]

2 OF PENTACLES

Qualities: Oscillation, Evolution, Progression
Inversion: Stagnation, Devolution, Digression
Verse/s: ~ Ecclesiastes 3:1-8 (KJV) To every thing there is a season, and a time to every purpose under the heaven: A time to be born, and a time to die; a time to plant, and a time to pluck up that which is planted; A time to kill, and a time to heal; a time to break down, and a time to build up; A time to weep, and a time to laugh; a time to mourn, and a time to dance; A time to cast away stones, and a time to gather stones together; a time to embrace, and a time to refrain from embracing; A time to get, and a time to lose; a time to keep, and a time to cast away; A time to rend, and a time to sew; a time to keep silence, and a time to speak; A time to love, and a time to hate; a time of war, and a time of peace.

~ Heraclitus (c. 535–475 BCE), pre-Socratic Greek philosopher: "You cannot step twice into the same river."[48]

ACE OF PENTACLES

Qualities: Renewal, Genesis, Incarnation
Inversion: Decay, Harvest, Excarnation
Angel: רָפָאֵל ~ Raphael ~ إسرافيل ~ Isrāfīl
Verse/s: ~ Tobit 12:6-7 (NABRE) Raphael called the two of them aside privately and said to them: "Bless God and give him thanks before all the living for the good things he has done for you, by blessing and extolling his name in song. Proclaim before all with due honor the deeds of God, and do not be slow to acknowledge him. It is good to conceal the secret of a king, but to reveal and acknowledge the works of God is honorable. Do good, and evil will not overtake you."[49]

~ Surah Az-Zumar 39:68 (Pickthall) And the trumpet is blown, and all who are in the heavens and all who are in the earth swoon, save him whom Allah willeth. Then it is blown a second time, and lo! they stand up, looking on.

SUGGESTED RESOURCES

- Chang, T. Susan, and M. M. Meleen. Tarot Deciphered: Decoding Esoteric Symbols in the Major Arcana. Newburyport, MA: Red Wheel/Weiser, 2021.
- Anonymous. Meditations on the Tarot: A Journey into Christian Hermeticism. Translated by Robert A. Powell. New York: Jeremy P. Tarcher/Penguin, 2002.
- Cicero, Chic, and Sandra Tabatha Cicero. Self-Initiation into the Golden Dawn Tradition: A Complete Curriculum of Study for Both the Solitary Magician and the Working Magical Group. St. Paul, MN: Llewellyn Publications, 1995.
- Crowley, Aleister. The Book of Thoth: A Short Essay on the Tarot of the Egyptians. New York: Samuel Weiser, 1969. (Original limited edition: 1944; this is the standard accessible reprint.)
- Flowers, Stephen E. The Magian Tarok: The Origins of the Tarot in the Mithraic and Hermetic Traditions. Revised and expanded edition. Rochester, VT: Inner Traditions / Destiny Books, 2019. ISBN 978-1620558690.
- Al-Buni, Ahmad ibn 'Ali. The Sun of Knowledge (Shams al-Ma'arif): An Arabic Grimoire in Selected Translation. Translated by Amina Inloes, with commentary and illustrations by J.M. Hamade. Newburyport, MA: Revelore Press, 2022.
- Kaplan, Aryeh. Sefer Yetzirah: The Book of Creation in Theory and Practice. York Beach, ME: Samuel

Weiser, 1997. (Revised edition; original publication
1990.)

BIBLIOGRAPHY

1.   Al-Būnī, Aḥmad ibn ʿAlī. Shams al-Maʿārif al-Kubrā. Beinecke MS 32304220, fol. 54a. Beinecke Rare Book & Manuscript Library, Yale University.

2.   Crowley, Aleister. The Book of the Law (Liber AL vel Legis). 1904. York Beach, ME: Weiser Books, 2004.

3.   Crowley, Aleister. The Book of Thoth (Egyptian Tarot). London: O.T.O., 1944. Reprint, New York: Samuel Weiser, 1969.

4.   Betz, Hans Dieter, ed. The Greek Magical Papyri in Translation, Including the Demotic Spells. 2nd ed. Chicago: University of Chicago Press, 1992.

5.   Crowley, Aleister. 777 and Other Qabalistic Writings of Aleister Crowley: Including Gematria & Sepher Sephiroth. Edited and introduced by Israel Regardie. York Beach, ME: Samuel Weiser, 1973.

6.   Regardie, Israel. The Golden Dawn: The Original Account of the Teachings, Rites, and Ceremonies of the Hermetic Order. 7th ed., revised and corrected by John Michael Greer. Woodbury, MN: Llewellyn Publications, 2016.

7.   Anonymous. Meditations on the Tarot: A Journey into Christian Hermeticism. Translated by Robert A. Powell. New York: Jeremy P. Tarcher/Penguin, 2002.

8.   Kamen, Roy Kenneth. Karate: Beneath The Surface: Emotional Content of Kata. [Self-published / Kamen Entertainment Group, Inc.], 2017. ISBN 978-0999042700.

9.   Chang, T. Susan, and Mel Meleen, hosts. Fortune's Wheelhouse. Podcast. 2017–2021.

10.   Al-Bukhari, Muhammad ibn Isma'il. Sahih al-Bukhari. Hadith 7017 (Book 81, Hadith 1385 in older numbering). Translated by Muhammad Muhsin Khan. Riyadh: Darussalam, 1997.

11.   King, Karen L. The Gospel of Mary of Magdala: Jesus and the First Woman Apostle. Polebridge Press, 2003.

12.   Al-Bukhari, Muhammad ibn Isma'il. Sahih al-Bukhari. Hadith 3 (or 7017 in modern numbering). Translated by Muhammad Muhsin Khan. Riyadh: Darussalam, 1997.

13.   al-Ṭabarī, Muḥammad ibn Jarīr. Tārīkh al-Rusul wa-al-Mulūk. Edited by M. J. de Goeje et al. 15 vols. Leiden: Brill, 1879–1901. See the relevant section on the revelation of Surah al-Najm (53:19–23) and the alleged gharāniq incident. For the underlying tradition from Ibn Isḥāq, see Ibn Hishām, Sīrat Rasūl Allāh, translated by Alfred Guillaume as The Life of Muhammad: A Translation of Isḥāq's Sīrat Rasūl Allāh (Karachi: Oxford University Press, 1955), 165–166.

14.   Foster, Benjamin R. Reading Akkadian Prayers and Hymns: An Introduction. Atlanta: Society of Biblical Literature, 2011.

15.   Al-Bukhari, Muhammad ibn Isma'il. Sahih al-Bukhari. Hadith 4281. Book 64 (Military Expeditions led by the Prophet), Hadith 315.

16.   Al-Bukhari, Muhammad ibn Isma'il. Sahih al-Bukhari. Hadith 1904. Translated by Muhammad Muhsin Khan.

17.   Al-Bukhārī, Muḥammad ibn Ismā'īl. Ṣaḥīḥ al-Bukhārī. Hadith 6114 (Book 78: Good Manners and Form). Narrated by Abu Hurairah.

18.   Al-Qushayrī, Muslim ibn al-Ḥajjāj. Ṣaḥīḥ Muslim. Hadith 1599 (Book 22: The Book of Government). Narrated by an-Nu'mān ibn Bashīr.

19.   Muslim ibn al-Ḥajjāj al-Qushayrī al-Naysābūrī. Ṣaḥīḥ Muslim. Translated by Abdul Hamid Siddiqui. Riyadh: Darussalam, n.d. See especially Book 1, Hadith 164 (91a).

20.   Al-Tha'labi, Ahmad ibn Ibrahim. Qisas al-Anbiya'. Cairo: Dar al-Kutub al-'Ilmiyyah (or relevant edition). Section on Bilqis (Queen of Sheba). Chain: Said ibn Bashir ← Qatadah ← An-Nadr ibn Anas ← Bashir ibn Nahik ← Abu Hurairah.

21.   Muhammad Muhsin Khan (trans.). Sahih al-Bukhari. Riyadh: Darussalam, n.d. Book 6 (Menstrual Periods), Hadith 297.

22.   al-Bukhārī, Muḥammad ibn Ismā'īl. Ṣaḥīḥ al-Bukhārī. Edited by Muḥammad Zuhayr ibn Nāṣir al-Nāṣir. Vol. 8. Riyadh: Dār al-Salām, 1997. Hadith no. 6324.

23.   al-Tirmidhī, Sunan al-Tirmidhī, hadith no. 2346 (Hasan), ed. Shu'ayb al-Arna'ūṭ (Beirut: Mu'assasat al-Risālah, 1998).

24.   Muḥammad ibn Ismā'īl al-Bukhārī. Ṣaḥīḥ al-Bukhārī. Translated by Muhammad Muhsin Khan. Riyadh: Darussalam, n.d. (Book 8 [Prayers (Salat)], Hadith 519).

25.   Sun Tzu. The Art of War. Translated by Lionel Giles. Chapter 7. London: Luzac & Co., 1910. Reprint, New York: Dover Publications, 2002.

26.   Kingdom of Heaven. Directed by Ridley Scott, screenplay by William Monahan. 20th Century Fox, 2005.

27.   Kipling, Rudyard. "If—." Rewards and Fairies. London: Macmillan, 1910.

28.   Roosevelt, Theodore. "Citizenship in a Republic." Speech at the Sorbonne, Paris, April 23, 1910.

29.   Muslim ibn al-Hajjaj al-Qushayri. Sahih Muslim. Hadith 199. Book 1: The Book of Faith (Kitab al-Iman). Narrated by Abu Hurairah.

30.   Ibn Mājah, Muḥammad ibn Yazīd. Sunan Ibn Mājah. Hadith 238 (Book of the Sunnah). Narrated by Sahl bin Saʿd. Graded ḍaʿīf.

31.   al-Bukhārī, Muḥammad ibn Ismāʿīl. Ṣaḥīḥ al-Bukhārī. Translated by Muhammad Muhsin Khan. Riyadh: Darussalam, n.d. (Book 34 [Sales and Trade], Hadith 2072).

32.   Denver, Rorke, with Ellis Henican. Damn Few: Making the Modern SEAL Warrior. New York: Hachette Books, 2013.

33.   Muslim ibn al-Ḥajjāj al-Qushayrī. Ṣaḥīḥ Muslim. Translated by Abdul Hamid Siddiqui. Lahore: Sh. Muhammad Ashraf, n.d. (Book 12 [The Book of Faith], Hadith 1048a).

34.   At-Tirmidhī, Muḥammad ibn ʿĪsā. Jāmiʿ at-Tirmidhī. Hadith 2000 (Book of Manners). Narrated by Abu Hurairah.

35.   al-Tirmidhī, Muḥammad ibn ʿĪsá. Jāmiʿ al-Tirmidhī. Translated by Abu Khaliyl. Riyadh: Darussalam, n.d. (Book 49 [Chapters on Virtues], Hadith 3880).

36.   Ibn Hanbal, Ahmad. Musnad Ahmad. Vol. 4, Hadith approx. 171-173 (narration via Yaʿla ibn

Murrah). Graded Sahih. Sunnah-related compilations and al-Hakim's al-Mustadrak (2:617).

37.   Charles, R. H. The Book of Enoch or 1 Enoch: Translated from the Editor's Ethiopic Text. Oxford: Clarendon Press, 1912. (Chapter 8, verses 1-3).

38.   Herbert, Frank. Dune. Philadelphia: Chilton Books, 1965. (Litany Against Fear).

39.   al-Bukhārī, Muḥammad ibn Ismā'īl. Ṣaḥīḥ al-Bukhārī. Translated by Muhammad Muhsin Khan. Riyadh: Darussalam, n.d. (Book 23 [Funerals], Hadith 1284).

40.   Abu Dawud Sulayman ibn al-Ash'ath al-Sijistani. Sunan Abi Dawud. Translated by Ahmad Hasan. Riyadh: Darussalam, n.d. (Book 28 [Foods], Hadith 3851).

41.   Tolkien, J.R.R. The Return of the King: Being the Third Part of The Lord of the Rings. Boston: Houghton Mifflin, 1955.

42.   Muslim ibn al-Ḥajjāj al-Qushayrī. Ṣaḥīḥ Muslim. Translated by Abdul Hamid Siddiqui. Lahore: Sh. Muhammad Ashraf, n.d. (Book 55 [The Book of Remembrance, Supplication, Repentance and Seeking Forgiveness], Hadith 2729).

43.   Apollo 13. Directed by Ron Howard. Universal Pictures, 1995.

44.   Plutarch. Moralia. Translated by Frank Cole Babbitt. Vol. 3. Loeb Classical Library 245. Cambridge, MA: Harvard University Press, 1931. "Sayings of Spartan Women," 241F.

45.   Al-Bukhari, Muhammad ibn Isma'il. Sahih al-Bukhari. Hadith 6064. Book 78: Good Manners and Form (Al-Adab), Hadith 94. Narrated by Abu Huraira.

46.   Confucius (Kongzi). The Analects. Translated by D.C. Lau. London: Penguin Classics, 1979.

47.   al-Bukhārī, Muḥammad ibn Ismāʿīl. Ṣaḥīḥ al-Bukhārī. Translated by Muhammad Muhsin Khan. Riyadh: Darussalam, n.d. (Book 1 [Revelation], Hadith 6496).

48.   Heraclitus. Fragment B91 (Diels-Kranz numbering). In The Presocratic Philosophers, edited by G.S. Kirk, J.E. Raven, and M. Schofield, 2nd ed., 197. Cambridge: Cambridge University Press, 1983.

49.   New American Bible Revised Edition. Confraternity of Christian Doctrine. Washington, DC: United States Conference of Catholic Bishops, 2011.

SCRIPTURAL SOURCES

The Holy Quran. Translated by Muhammad Marmaduke Pickthall. The Meaning of the Glorious Quran. London: George Allen & Unwin, 1930.

The Holy Bible. King James Version (KJV). 1611

ABOUT THE AUTHOR

ʿĀʾishah bint Maniyyah, born in the early 1980's, was raised in southern California in a loosely Christian household. Although her home life was not strongly affected by Christian theology, ʿĀʾishah attended a Christ-centric elementary school for several years where her first deep connection to the faith of Abraham as affirmed by Christ was established. Common for many raised in 'Christian' families that were not strongly devout, ʿĀʾishah spent several years somewhat disconnected from religion. In her youth and early adulthood ʿĀʾishah had also dabbled in the martial arts. In 2012 AD, however, concurrent with many dramatic life changing events, ʿĀʾishah began training heavily with her Teacher/Sensei in the Japanese martial arts where she currently holds the rank of Sandan/3rd degree black belt in Koei Kan Karate Do.

After tasting both spiritual bliss and hellfire while journeying on the path of the Budo, - the Martial

Way - ʿĀʾishah struggled to find appropriate terminology with which to articulate her spiritual encounters, especially from within the paradigm of traditional Christian ideology. ʿĀʾishah, while sojourning through a dark night of the soul experience, re-encountered Christ and became enthralled with some of the more esoteric teachings found in the gnostic Christian materials - often considered heretical by the Orthodoxy. ʿĀʾishah continued to expand her scope of study while attempting to claw her way out of the abyss and break out of the box of dogmatic conditioning - such as the notion that even questioning seemingly contradictory doctrine within the mainstream religion was grounds for eternal damnation.

Some materials examined ranged from books regarding the Depth Psychology of Carl Jung, to those covering traditions considered completely antithetical to Christ - particularly, though not limited to, brilliant works by Aleister Crowley as well as multiple writings composed by the Temple of Set founder, Dr. Michael Aquino. Through this course of study insight was gleaned regarding mysteries that had been taught by Christ though not extrapolated upon within the framework of mainstream Christian doctrine. Additionally, a more appropriate working vocabulary was accumulated to better accommodate the wide range of phenomena encountered in the Budo.

Before closing, we may touch upon two additional elements that became crucial to the formation of this work. Growing up in the West, Islam had not often been painted in a positive light and had not been taught as being complementary to Christianity. Rather than listen solely to hearsay, ʿĀʾishah went directly to the source and read the Quran. Feeling called by Christ to do so, she began observing some of the core practices of the faith while becoming more immersed in the teachings of the Prophet Muhammad ﷺ. In like manner to the clarity provided by certain of the gnostic materials regarding the teachings of Christ; the wisdom in the Quran seemed to elucidate, confirm, and expand upon them all.

Finally, although considered demonic or haram/forbidden by many following mainstream interpretations of Christianity and Islam; ʿĀʾishah found that encapsulated within the Tarot were spiritual and philosophical teachings passed down since time immemorial. From Jungian Archetypes, to the fool's/hero's journey and Alchemy, Hermeticism, Qabalah, esoteric Christianity and Islam, martial philosophy, astrology, mysticism, magick, the light, the dark, polarity, plurality, and unity all within a deck of cards. From ʿĀʾishah's journeys in the underworld and moments in the light, the People of the Night Tarot was borne.

Notes:

Notes:

---

www.ingramcontent.com/pod-product-compliance
Lightning Source LLC
Chambersburg PA
CBHW071952150726

47999CB00001B/419